Restoring Opportunity

Restoring Opportunity

*The Crisis of Inequality
and the Challenge for
American Education*

Greg J. Duncan and
Richard J. Murnane

HARVARD EDUCATION PRESS
CAMBRIDGE, MASSACHUSETTS

RUSSELL SAGE FOUNDATION
NEW YORK, NEW YORK

Third Printing, 2015

Copyright © 2014 by the President and Fellows of Harvard College and the Russell Sage Foundation

All rights reserved. No part of this publication may be reproduced or transmitted in any form or by any means, electronic or mechanical, including photocopy, recording, or any information storage and retrieval systems, without permission in writing from the publisher.

Library of Congress Control Number 2013949344

Paperback ISBN 978-1-61250-634-0
Library Edition ISBN 978-1-61250-635-7

Published by Harvard Education Press,
an imprint of the Harvard Education Publishing Group,
and the Russell Sage Foundation

Harvard Education Press
8 Story Street
Cambridge, MA 02138
www.harvardeducationpress.org

Russell Sage Foundation
112 East 64th Street
New York, NY 10065
www.russellsage.org

Cover Design: Steven Pisano
Cover photo: Ocean/Corbis

The typefaces used in this book are Minion Pro and ITC Stone Sans.

To Dorothy and Mary Jo

Contents

1   A Fading Dream   1

2   Diverging Destinies   7

3   Family Income and School Success   23

4   Challenges in the Classroom   35

5   Promising Prekindergarten Programs   53

6   Elementary Schools That Work   71

7   High Schools That Improve Life Chances   85

8   Programs That Support Families   109

9   Restoring Opportunity   123

Notes   145

Acknowledgments   173

About the Authors   177

Index   179

1

A Fading Dream

AMERICANS WANT TO BELIEVE that ours is a land of opportunity, where no matter what a person's starting point, those who work hard—and their kids—can "make it." For much of the twentieth century, economic growth made that dream a reality for generations of Americans. This was particularly evident in the thirty years following the end of World War II, when both the economy and the incomes of families at the top and the bottom of the income ladder doubled in size.

Fueling much of this growth was an increasingly educated work force.[1] Average schooling increased by six years between 1900 and 1970, with growing numbers of children completing more education than their parents. This, coupled with technological advances that benefited both high- and low-skilled workers, led to widely shared increases in living standards and intergenerational mobility.

But storm clouds began to gather in the 1970s. In contrast to the first three-quarters of the twentieth century, the last quarter saw computer-driven technological advances that rewarded skills that only the most educated Americans possessed. Moreover, many manufacturing jobs began to be outsourced to low-wage countries. These trends, continuing into the twenty-first century, have translated into substantial growth in the wages of college graduates, no growth in the wages of high school graduates, and falling wages for high school dropouts. As a consequence, the living standards of children in higher-income families have risen while the incomes of low-income children have stagnated or even declined.

One might have hoped that the increasing monetary rewards associated with college-level skills would have spurred large increases in educational attainment. But this has not happened. Beginning in the 1970s, high school graduation rates stalled for several decades. Today, the United States no longer leads the world in high school and college graduation rates. Fewer children are exceeding their parents' schooling levels. Gaps in academic skills and educational attainments between low- and higher-income American children have grown sharply.

Why is the American Dream of upward mobility fading? Historically, this country has relied on its public schools to help level the playing field for children born into different circumstances. But those schools are no longer able to ameliorate the effects of inequality—and may inadvertently be exacerbating them. As we will explain in more detail in the chapters that follow, the macroeconomic forces that have driven a widening wedge between the incomes of affluent families and those of poor and working-class families have also made it much more difficult for schools to help children from low-income families acquire the skills they need to compete in today's economy. Changes in the ways that families at different ends of the income spectrum use their money and time have helped transform income gaps into achievement gaps. At the same time, increasing residential segregation based on income is widening the quality gap between the schools that low- and higher-income children attend while compounding the unique problems faced by high-poverty schools. Demographic patterns, such as increases in immigration and in the number of single-parent families, also play a role. All of these are forces that are beyond the control of schools but that affect schools greatly.

The story of the diverging destinies of American school children could be told solely with charts and graphs, and we have included much information of this type throughout the book. However, we also draw from previously published accounts of four boys from different families, different neighborhoods, and different economic backgrounds to paint a fuller picture of how and why these educational disparities have grown. The stories of Anthony, Alexander, Garrett, and Harold, whom you will meet in chapters 2 and 3, are taken from research by sociologist Annette Lareau. Between 1989 and 1995, Lareau and her research team studied white and African American fourth graders from widely different economic backgrounds, paying nearly daily visits to the families of selected students for three weeks and revisiting them once they reached adulthood. The lives of the four boys we chose to feature in this book illustrate some of the disparities wrought by recent economic, social, and familial changes. Their divergent destinies, described in the chapters that follow, have been shaped by macroeconomic forces that have driven a widening wedge between the incomes of the millions of families toward the top of the income scale and the millions of poor and working-class families toward the bottom.[2]

Stagnant educational attainments and growing inequality in educational outcomes call into question America's vision of itself as a land of growth and opportunity. But the purpose of this book is not simply to document the problem. In the second half of the book we focus on successful schools and programs that show that it is possible to provide children from low-income families with the opportunities they need to have a fair shot at achieving the American Dream of upward mobility.

A quick look inside one elementary classroom, located in a charter school on Chicago's South Side, suggests what schools that provide these kinds of opportunities look like. All of the twenty-seven children in Shannon Keys's second-grade class are African American and live in low-income neighborhoods of the city. A visit to her classroom finds the students working in groups at one of several activity centers. The group work is designed to teach children the interactive skills that are essential for many middle-class jobs. All of the activities build in some way on E. B. White's *The Trumpet of the Swan,* which Keys has been reading to her class. At the writing center, children are answering questions designed to help them make inferences from what they have heard and to encourage them to defend their conclusions using supporting evidence. At the poetry center, they are reading poems aloud to a partner, following the guidelines for fluent reading posted on the wall. At the ABC center, students are writing definitions, synonyms, and antonyms for the word "coy," which is taken from *The Trumpet of the Swan.* Building children's vocabulary and background knowledge is important, as these skills are critical for making sense of science and social studies texts in the upper elementary grades.

After a few minutes, the teacher's aide rings a bell and each group moves quietly to the next activity center, following the instructions Keys posts on the Center Board each morning. Of course, this orderly transition did not come naturally to the seven-year-olds in the class. Keys and the entire school staff worked to develop these routines during the first six weeks of school, a period she calls Boot Camp. Each week Keys introduced a new activity center, modeled the work to be done there, and provided ample opportunities for the children to practice both the work and appropriate group behaviors. Instructional time is a precious resource, and during Boot Camp the children need to learn how to make the best use of it to enhance their learning and that of their classmates.

The professional life of Keys and her colleagues is shaped by two complementary principles: support and accountability. Support comes in a variety of forms, all of which are critical to the success of the school. For Keys, support includes help in implementing a rich, complex literacy curriculum consistently and effectively. This support was so important to Keys that she left a better-paying job to take advantage of the opportunities the charter school offered for her to grow as a teacher. Accountability involves demonstrating progress toward the goal of having all students meet state standards. More immediately, accountability means Keys's acceptance of a shared responsibility to her colleagues and parents to educate every student well. As we illustrate throughout the book, support and accountability are not alternative strategies for improving schools. Neither, by itself, will do the job. Together, however, consistent school supports and well-designed accountability are essential building blocks for producing a system of effective schools.

In chapters 5 through 7 we show how the twin forces of support and accountability play out in the daily lives of teachers and students, first in Boston's public prekindergarten program, then in a network of charter schools on Chicago's South Side, and finally in small high schools in New York City. We explain why these complementary principles are central to the success of educational programs that are improving the life chances of a great many low-income children. In chapter 8 we describe a successful family work-support program that also incorporates these principles.

Throughout the book, we focus on proven initiatives. All have been evaluated using state-of-the-art methods, and the evaluations provide compelling evidence not just that these initiatives have worked, but that they have done so for a significant number of years. The educational programs we highlight are truly exceptional, but they also show what is possible in American education today. In each case we explain why the education in these schools works and contrast it with the education most low-income children currently experience.

The hurdles to implementing serious reforms in our classrooms are high. As a nation, we have failed to appreciate the extent to which technological changes over the past several decades have altered the skills needed to succeed in today's economy. Moreover, the rising economic and social inequality produced by technology and globalization has weakened neighborhoods and families in ways that make effective school reform that much more difficult. For a variety of historical reasons we will discuss, our nation has not learned how to provide the consistent supports that schools and teachers, especially those serving large numbers of low-income children, must have to succeed.

In our final chapter we examine why Shannon Keys's charter school and the other programs we describe are the exception rather than the rule in the educational experiences of low-income children. Discussions of school reforms often center on simplistic "silver bullets"—more money, more accountability, more choice, new organizational structures. None of these reforms has turned the tide, because they fail to improve what matters most in education: the quality and consistency of the instruction and experiences offered to students.

We close by describing building blocks for an "American solution" to the serious problems facing our nation's schools. These include the new Common Core curriculum standards, consistent school supports, well-designed accountability, advances in knowledge, and, outside of school, programs that support low-income families' efforts to balance the demands of work and family.

The country's future prosperity, and our ability to make the dream of upward mobility a reality, depend on reversing a trend toward increasingly diverging destinies in the education and lives of high- and low-income children. The successful educational interventions we describe in this book demonstrate that we, as a nation, have learned and continue to learn a great deal about how to educate low-income students well. Yet our nation does this for only a small percentage of them. We hope this book will help galvanize a nationwide commitment to put this knowledge into action so that every child has the opportunity to succeed, despite the barriers and challenges faced by so many.

2

Diverging Destinies

ALL IN ALL, 1972 LOOKED LIKE a good year to graduate from high school. The Vietnam War still gripped the country, but both the war and the draft were about to end. The OPEC oil embargo was still a year away and the nation was enjoying not only cheap gasoline but also low inflation. Transistors were beginning to revolutionize computing, although in early 1972 handheld calculators often weighed two pounds, cost two hundred dollars, and could still perform only the four basic arithmetic functions.[1]

There was little need for high school graduates to worry if they wanted to pass up college and head directly into the labor market. The economy was recovering from a minor recession, with the unemployment rate headed below 5 percent. Even unemployment among teenagers was low.[2] To be sure, college graduates earned more than high school grads, but their 40 percent wage advantage was modest by historical standards and small enough that some would-be college students were no doubt convinced to change their plans.[3] Indeed, a book published in the middle of the decade, *The Overeducated American*, made headlines for concluding that the earnings payoff to higher education was declining.[4]

The year 1972 also marked the beginning of a landmark study of high school seniors. Some nineteen thousand students in the study were selected at random from more than one thousand schools.[5] For one-third of them, high school graduation would mark the end of their formal schooling.[6] But even their high school diplomas were an indication of the kind of intergenerational mobility that was a source of pride for most Americans;

7

nearly one-third of the graduates had already completed more schooling than either of their parents.[7]

Most of the male high school graduates would go on to begin promising careers. A follow-up survey conducted in 1979, when respondents were in their mid-twenties, found that more than 90 percent of the men with just a high school diploma were working full-time. Most held skilled blue-collar jobs and enjoyed earnings that were close to the national average.[8] These successes were hardly a surprise at the time, given that technology-driven productivity increases across the 1950s and 1960s had led to steep gains in the economic fortunes of both high- and low-skilled workers. Today we tend to think of technology in terms of the breathtaking advances made possible by microprocessors, nanotechnology, and biotechnology. But the broad sweep of the twentieth century included advances such as the introduction of electric power into homes and factories, assembly line production techniques, and the construction of the interstate highway system. These advances catalyzed economic growth and increased earnings opportunities for both highly educated workers and those with relatively little formal education.

Fueling the economic growth that resulted from these advances was America's remarkable support for universal secondary education and access to college for all who could qualify. The spectacular growth in schooling is shown in figure 2.1.[9] In 1890, the average fourteen-year-old ended up completing fewer than eight years of school. Educational attainments increased steadily for the next seventy years, with the early-wave baby boomers born shortly after World War II completing between thirteen and fourteen years of school, on average. These increases, coupled with technological progress, drove the economic progress that put American standards of living well ahead of virtually all other industrialized countries. Indeed, the picture was so rosy that few people suspected that America's stellar track record of upward intergenerational mobility was about to take a sharp turn for the worse.[10]

In fact, a perfect storm was brewing to sink the labor market prospects of workers with modest educational attainments. The recession in the early 1980s would become the worst downturn since the Great Depression.

Figure 2.1   Years of schooling completed by U.S. adults

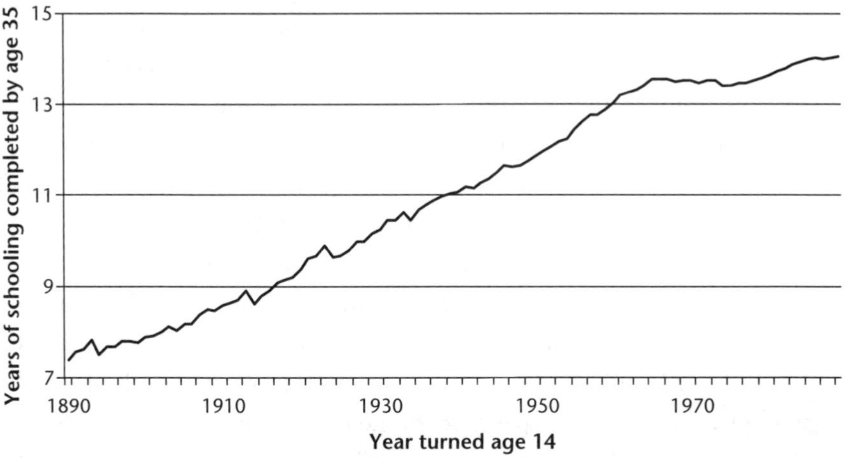

Source: Adapted from figure 1.4 in Claudia D. Goldin and Lawrence F. Katz, *The Race Between Education and Technology* (Cambridge, MA: Belknap Press of Harvard University Press, 2008).

But much larger forces would prove even more important. In particular, technological changes came to be dominated by advances in computers, which were becoming ever smaller, less expensive, and more powerful. In the decades to come, this change would link educational attainment and earnings more tightly than ever before.

The microprocessor revolution dealt a double blow to the less educated. Whereas prior technological advances had boosted the earnings of both college- and high-school educated workers, computer-based technological advances fueled the demand for highly educated workers alone, while simultaneously reducing the demand for workers hired for routine tasks such as bookkeeping and much of assembly-line production work. These tasks, which had previously provided jobs for many high school graduates, have been the easiest for computers or computer-driven machinery to take over.

Moreover, advances in telecommunication have made it increasingly possible for American companies to offshore to lower-wage countries many of the tasks that American workers, especially those without college training, had performed in the past. The net result has been that a growing number of high school graduates now find themselves competing for service jobs such as preparing and serving food and caring for the elderly. While the number of jobs in many service occupations is growing because the work is difficult to computerize or send offshore, the pay is low because there is an ample supply of workers vying for these jobs.[11]

Anthony Mears is one of those earning that low pay.[12] At age twenty, with just a high school degree, Anthony has found a job working for $12 an hour at a construction job in lead abatement, thanks to the help of a friend. He aspires to start a business in home remodeling and real estate, but those prospects seem remote. By earning a high school diploma, Anthony has already completed more education than his father and grandfathers. But unfortunately, Anthony grew up at a time when a high school diploma was no longer the passport to the middle class.

Born in the mid-1980s and growing up in a working-class urban neighborhood, Anthony experienced a childhood much like that of his parents. He spent most of his considerable free time playing made-up games with his fourth-grade friends, with no adults in sight. One of his favorites involved calling out a command (touch your toes, clap three times) to follow between ball bounces. Like many boys his age, Anthony and his friends spent an inordinate amount of time haggling over the rules, devising new ones, and settling disputes. However, unlike many more affluent children, Anthony and his friends did so without the intervention of a coach or another adult. That's not to say there was no oversight. Anthony's mother set strict rules for him and his older sister. He had to finish his homework before he could go out and play, he had to stay within his neighborhood, and he had to return home when called. But within these boundaries, he and his friends were free to play or invent whatever games appealed to them.

In the context of the early 1990s, Anthony's family enjoyed a degree of working-class financial stability that others in his neighborhood—a stable working-class black neighborhood with its fair share of crime—did not. His mother earned about $30,000 a year (in 2012 dollars) as a secretary and managed her company's fleet of cars. Her job provided health insurance and allowed the family to rent a four-bedroom home. Anthony's parents were divorced, but his father saw his children regularly, and though he did not pay child support, he did help out, when he could, when the children needed things like clothing.

Family income was high enough to put food on the table and finance weekly trips to a fast-food restaurant and monthly trips to the local Sizzler steakhouse, but these little luxuries depleted an emergency fund meant to cover unexpected bills and keep the family car running. The family managed to take a vacation at the beach every summer, but only because Anthony's mother put in extra hours at work to cover the additional expense.

Anthony's parents struggled to keep his schooling on track. In elementary school, he had been a well-behaved student and earned mostly Bs and Cs. When it was time for high school, he initially enrolled in a charter school but yearned to play on the basketball team with his friends in his local public high school. His mother agreed to the switch but quickly regretted it, as Anthony spent much more time with his friends than on his studies and was even locked up briefly in juvenile hall. Desperate for a change, his mother pleaded successfully with Anthony's father for a $6,000 loan (she promised to repay half) to pay for private school for his senior year. Realizing that this was a considerable sacrifice for his parents, Anthony buckled down and managed to finish high school on time.

Like most blue-collar parents, Anthony's parents hoped that their sacrifices and support would allow their son to attend college and secure a middle-class job that would lead to a higher living standard than they were able to muster for themselves. Theirs was not a pie-in-the-sky hope. For many generations, most American children had achieved a higher standard of living than their parents, and rising educational attainments were the mechanism that made this possible. This did not happen in Anthony's case. Neither Anthony's parents nor his school pushed him to take the SAT college entrance exam. While his parents were able to scrape together the $2,500 needed to pay for four community college classes, Anthony showed little motivation to acquire more education, and he fell short of earning enough credits for a two-year degree.

Forty years ago, Anthony's childhood of made-up games, haggles over rules, and a middling performance in school would have likely sufficed to earn him a job in a factory or at a shipyard—with job security and a living wage. Bypassing college would not come with a sizable penalty as it does today. He could have looked forward to a decent career with a fairly steady income. But today's world, as we will show, demands much more to succeed, from greater parental oversight to exposure to a wider range of adults and experiences, to more income so that parents are able to cultivate the skills, interests, and pursuits that help set a child apart in today's highly competitive economy.

Another boy, and another story, underscore the elements it takes to get ahead today in contrast to a generation ago. As a fourth-grader growing up around the same time as Anthony, Alexander Williams lived in a well-to-do community in a large northeastern city.[13] Like Anthony, Alexander and his parents are African American, as are most of the families in their neighborhood. Both of Alexander's parents are accomplished professionals; his mother is in management and his father is a lawyer specializing in medical malpractice cases. At that time, the family's combined yearly income exceeded $300,000 (in 2012 dollars), which paid for a large house with a spacious lawn as well as music lessons and private school for Alexander. Like Anthony's mother, Alexander's mother was devoted to her son's school success. But while Anthony's family finances were always tight, Alexander's parents enjoyed a level of financial security that allowed them to focus on providing their son with academic stimulation.

Alexander attended an academically demanding, mostly white private school from kindergarten through high school, but his parents made sure he was not the sole African American in his classes. Unlike Anthony, Alexander led a life that was chock-full of carefully chosen, adult-supervised activities—piano, choir, soccer, a school play—that kept him busy some days until nine o'clock at night.

Alexander's parents seized teachable moments at every opportunity. On Saturday mornings, when many kids were watching cartoons, Alexander and his mom were out of the house by 8:15 for a full day of "more productive" activities, as she called them. Alexander was raised to believe in his abilities. He also was taught the subtle people skills that are so important for getting ahead in life. At one medical checkup, he was confident enough to interrupt and correct the doctor. Alexander did very well in school—all A's, typically. He would later score 1350 out of a possible 1600 on the SAT college entrance test, and his achievements in high school would win him admission to a special eight-year program at an exclusive university that combines an undergraduate education with medical school.

Barring some unforeseen disaster, Alexander will assume his position in the upper middle class, as his parents have hoped and expected. But Anthony, unlike prior generations, risks not just remaining in the working class, like his parents, but slipping further down the social ladder. If Anthony had been born thirty years earlier, he would have walked into a factory job. But that world was disappearing by the time he was born.

As figure 2.2 shows, in 1979 blue-collar positions, most of which were in the manufacturing sector, accounted for nearly one-third of all jobs; by 2009, that share had shrunk to one-fifth.[14] Some white-collar occupations

Figure 2.2   Growth and decline of selected occupations

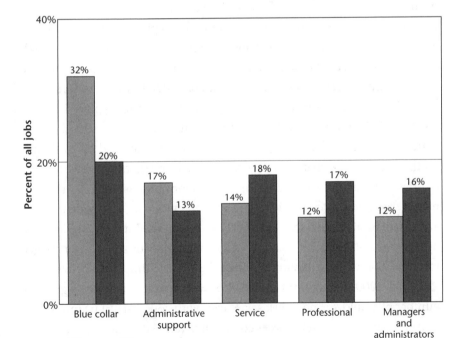

Source: Data provided by David Autor, Department of Economics, MIT, who tabulated the percentages from Current Population Surveys.

also diminished in importance as a result of computerization, in particular the filing clerk and administrative support jobs that had provided employment for many female high school graduates. And while the share of jobs in high-skilled occupations for professionals and managers has grown, so too has the share of jobs in low-skilled service occupations. In other words, the distribution of the nation's jobs has polarized, with a large decline in the share of jobs in blue-collar and administrative support positions—jobs that used to provide middle-class opportunities for generations of men and women with relatively low levels of education.[15]

Technological advances have also made a difference in the tasks workers in particular occupations carry out as well as in the educational credentials employers seek when hiring new workers. Consider, for example, the changing nature of secretarial work in recent decades. According to the U.S. Department of Labor's *Occupational Outlook Handbook* for 1976, "Secretaries relieve their employers of routine duties so they can work on more important matters."[16] And indeed, in 1976 many high-school-educated secretaries spent their entire work day typing. Yet with the advent of computer-based word processing, a growing number of professionals found that it made more sense to type their own letters and memos than to dictate them to secretaries. Advances in computer-based speech recognition enhanced this trend and drove down the demand for typists. Secretaries still exist, but their *Handbook* definition now includes the kind of fleet management tasks that were part of the secretarial job held by Anthony's mother: "Office automation and organizational restructuring have led secretaries to assume a wide range of new responsibilities once reserved for managerial and professional staff. Many secretaries now provide training and orientation to new staff, conduct research on the Internet, and learn to operate new office technologies."[17] Although Anthony's mother managed to get her job without having a college degree, the difference between the 1976 and 2000 descriptions makes it easy to understand why a growing number of employers now seek secretaries with college-level training.

At the same time, other forces contributed to the decline in the earnings of workers without postsecondary education. The overall share of unionized jobs in the American economy dropped, as did the inflation-adjusted value of the minimum wage, while the number of immigrants competing for low-skilled jobs rose sharply.[18] All of these factors played at least some role in the eroding labor-market position of workers with less education, but none was as important as technological change and globalization.[19]

The net effect of economic and demographic forces on the earnings of high school graduates and four-year-college graduates has been dramatic. Between 1979 and 1987, the inflation-adjusted earnings of male high school graduates plunged by 16 percent, while the earnings of college-educated workers rose by nearly 10 percent. In the following two decades, while Anthony and Alexander were growing up, the earnings of the less educated continued to fall, albeit more slowly, while the earnings of college graduates rose modestly.[20]

THE WIDENING GULF IN SCHOOLING OUTCOMES

Historically, the decisions young Americans make about enrolling in and completing college have been influenced by the labor market rewards of a college degree. When the payoff is high, young people flock to college. When it's not, they think twice. This helps to explain why college enrollments stagnated during the 1970s, a decade when the college–high school earnings differential was relatively modest. But it would also lead us to expect a rapid increase in college attendance among young Americans during the 1980s, when the college–high school earnings differential grew markedly. That did not happen. As shown in figure 2.1, the level of schooling eventually completed increased only very slowly for individuals who were adolescents in the 1980s, and this pattern of very slow growth has continued to this day, even though the earnings differential has remained high by historical standards. This threatens future prosperity because the skills of the labor force are a key determinant of the productivity of the economy.

Why the sluggish growth in the rate of college completion? College decisions are often based on the "payoff," but they must also take into account college costs and the ability of students to do college-level work. The sticker price of college has more than doubled in the last twenty years.[21] This has deterred many students from enrolling in and completing college, especially those whose parents, like Anthony's, lack the resources to pay a large share of the bill. While financial aid, including federally funded Pell Grants, has eased the financial crunch for many low-income students and their parents, others either lack awareness of available aid or are discouraged by the extremely complex federal financial aid application form.[22]

The second factor contributing to slower growth in the number of college graduates in recent decades is the weak academic preparation of many high school graduates. Just as the gap between affluent and low-income children in the ability to pay for college has increased, so too has the gap in academic preparation, as measured by reading and mathematics test scores. Using SAT-type score scales to track these trends, the math achievement gap among eighth graders in 1978 amounted to 96 points, roughly one standard deviation.[23] Since eighth-grade students typically learn the equivalent of about 25 to 30 SAT points in math or reading over the school year, the 96-point gap in 1978 was huge.[24]

Although test scores of low-income children increased modestly between 1978 and 2008, scores of high-income children rose much more rapidly, resulting in a 35-point *increase* in the gap.[25] In other words, in the last thirty years, the gap between the average scores of eighth-graders from high- and low-income families has increased by an amount equal to a year's worth of learning.

Given the importance of academic preparation in determining educational success, it should come as no surprise that growth in the income-based gap in children's reading and mathematics achievement has contributed to a growing gap in the rate of college completion (figure 2.3). A little more than one-third of students from affluent families who entered high school in the mid-1970s graduated from college. Among students from affluent families who entered high school about two decades later, the college graduation rate was 18 percentage points higher. In contrast, among children from low-income families, the graduation rate for the later cohort (9 percent) was only 4 percentage points higher than that of the earlier cohort (5 percent).[26]

Analysts differ in their assessments of the relative importance of college costs and academic preparation in explaining the increasing gulf between

Figure 2.3   College graduation rates for low- and high-income children

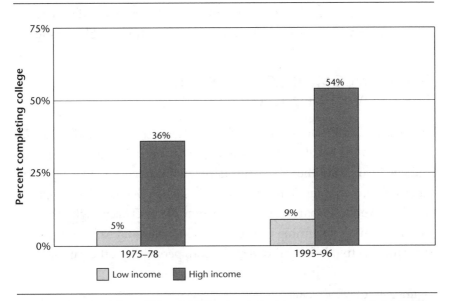

Source: Data based on Bailey and Dynarski (2011), who tabulated the percentages from National Longitudinal Survey of Youth files.

Note: Low and high incomes are defined as the bottom and top 25% of the parent income distribution. Dates indicate the calendar years in which the subjects turned age 14.

the college graduates rates of affluent and low-income children in our country.[27] However, as we explain in the next two chapters, both are rooted, at least in part, in the growth in family income inequality. For affluent children like Alexander Williams, whose families benefited the most from increasing incomes, college graduation rates jumped sharply. In contrast, very few children raised in low-income families graduated from college at any time during the last two decades. Anthony was no exception. As a result, children raised in higher-income families accounted for nearly all of the growth in college graduation rates. And it is important to stress that our classification of high- and low-income families does not include only the superrich and desperately poor; each of our groups encompasses nearly twenty million American children, and together they include half of all children.[28]

Thus all of the achievement and attainment data point to the same conclusion: the slowdown in the rate of growth of educational attainments of

American young adults coincides with a growing divergence in educational outcomes between children from higher- and lower-income families. We now turn to some of the forces that have produced this troubling pattern.

FAMILY INCOME INEQUALITY AND THE GROWING EDUCATION GAP

The quarter century following World War II was a golden era for the U.S. economy, as the benefits of economic growth were shared by both high- and low-income families.[29] In contrast, economic changes favoring highly educated workers, plus demographic shifts such as the rise of single-parent families, produced sharply growing income gaps between high- and low-income families beginning in the 1970s. The left-hand bars in figure 2.4 show income trends for children at the 20th percentile of the nation's fam-

Figure 2.4 Children's family income over time

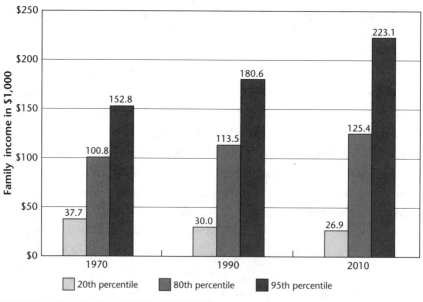

Note: Chart shows 20th, 80th, and 95th percentiles of the distribution of family incomes for all children age 5–17, based on data from the U.S. Bureau of the Census and adjusted for inflation. Amounts are in 2012$.

ily income distribution.[30] This means that, in a given year, 20 percent of children lived in families with incomes below that level while 80 percent had incomes above it. In 1970, the dividing line was drawn at $37,664 (in 2012 dollars). We refer to this group as "low income" rather than "poor" because it includes many families with incomes above the poverty line. Many of the children in this group have working parents.[31]

The middle bars show the trend in family incomes at the 80th percentile of the distribution, which was about $100,000 (in 2012 dollars) in 1970. The right-hand bars show the trend for very high-income families—those with incomes higher than 95 percent of U.S. families (a little more than about $150,000 in 1970 in 2012 dollars).

In contrast to the two decades before 1970, when the incomes of these three groups grew at virtually identical rates, economic growth over the next four decades failed to lift all boats. The family income (net of inflation) at the 20th percentile was more than 25 percent lower in 2010 than it was in 1970. In contrast, the incomes of families at the 80th percentile were 24 percent higher in 2010 ($125,000) than they were in 1970, while the incomes of the richest 5 percent of families rose even more over this period.[32] The decline of the incomes of families at the lower end of the spectrum is also reflected in the nation's child poverty rate, which at 21.9 percent in 2011 was up sharply from 15.1 percent in 1970.[33]

The simple consequence of these changes is that high-income families had a lot more money to spend on their children while the purchasing power of families on the lower rungs of the income ladder declined. All of these advantages can translate into increased school success for children from high-income families.

SCHOOLING AND INTERGENERATIONAL MOBILITY

Although the nation has never fulfilled the promise of offering equal educational opportunity to all, the openness of the American educational system made it possible for generations of hard-working children from low-income families to obtain more education than their parents had. The skills and credentials resulting from these educational investments provided the means for many Americans who had grown up poor to join the middle class. By the mid-twentieth century, more than one-half of young adult men and women had completed more years of education than their parents, a percentage that would continue to grow for the next twenty-five years (figure 2.5).[34] But that trend would come to a halt and then decline steadily through the 1990s.

Because education has been the dominant pathway to upward intergenerational mobility in the United States, the growing gap in educational attainments between children from low- and upper-income families is likely to perpetuate income inequality in future generations and undermine the mobility that has been a central part of the American Dream.[35] Taken together, changes in the economy, greater income inequality, and low-quality education for a great many low-income children pose a serious threat to the upward intergenerational mobility of which Americans have been so proud.

While educational attainments have stagnated in the United States, especially for children from low-income families, in many other countries

Figure 2.5 Trends in intergenerational mobility

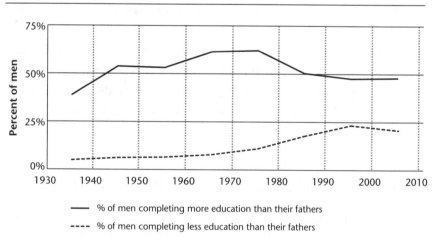

— % of men completing more education than their fathers

---- % of men completing less education than their fathers

Source: Hout and Janus in Duncan, Greg J., and Richard J. Murnane, eds. Figure 8.3, "Percentage Upwardly and Downwardly Mobile by Year Turned Twenty-Five and Gender: U.S.-Educated Persons, Twenty Seven to Sixty-Four Years Old at Time of Interview." p. 173. In *Whither Opportunity.* © 2011 Russell Sage Foundation, 112 East 641 Street, New York, NY 10065. Reprinted with permission.

Note: Dates indicate the calendar years in which the subjects turned age 14.

this has not been the case. Since education plays such an important role in intergenerational mobility, it is not surprising that there is greater upward economic mobility in the United Kingdom, the Nordic countries, and many continental European countries than in our country.[36]

Given the magnitude of the economic and demographic disruptions of the past forty years, it will not be easy to restore the degree of shared prosperity and upward intergenerational mobility that American children used to enjoy, and in particular to make education once again a force that reduces inequality rather than reinforcing it. However, it is possible to improve education for low-income children and to support their families. To appreciate what it will take to make education part of the solution, we need to understand the roles both families and schools have played in increasing the gap between the educational outcomes of affluent and low-income children. We turn to these topics in the next two chapters.

3

Family Income
and School Success

A SNAPSHOT OF Alexander Williams and Anthony Mears at age twenty finds them on strikingly different educational and, in all likelihood, career trajectories. Alexander appears well on his way to an Ivy League degree and medical school. Anthony has a job, but the recent violent deaths of two friends have him just hoping that he will still be alive in five years.

It is easy to imagine how the childhood circumstances of these two young men may have shaped their fates. Alexander lived in the suburbs while Anthony lived in the city center. Most of Alexander's suburban neighbors lived in families with incomes above the $125,000 that now separates the richest 20 percent of children from the rest. Anthony Mears's school served pupils from families whose incomes were near or below the $27,000 threshold separating the bottom 20 percent (see figure 2.4).

With an income of more than $300,000, Alexander's family was able to spend far more money on Alexander's education, lessons, and other enrichment activities than Anthony's parents could devote to their son's needs. Both of Alexander's parents had professional degrees, so they knew all about what Alexander needed to do to prepare himself for college. Anthony's mother completed some classes after graduating from high school, but his father, a high school dropout, struggled even to read. And in contrast to Anthony, Alexander lived with both of his parents, which not only added to family income but also increased the amount of time available for a parent to spend with Alexander.

Which of these factors are most powerful in determining a child's success in school? While Annette Lareau and her team did not monitor school progress or behavioral development for the children in her study, including Anthony and Alexander, many national studies have investigated gaps in school performance among children from similarly disparate backgrounds. As shown in chapter 2, math and reading gaps between high- and low-income children have grown substantially over the past three decades. Data from a recent national study of children who entered kindergarten in the fall of 1998 allow for a more detailed look at income-based gaps as children progress through school (figure 3.1).[1] As before, a 100-point difference in figure 3.1 corresponds to one standard deviation. Each bar shows the relative size of the gap between high- and low-income children.

Figure 3.1   Skill and behavior gaps between high- and low-income kindergarteners and fifth graders

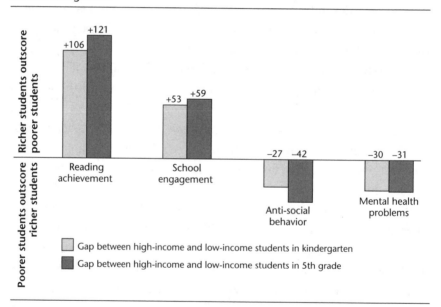

Source: Authors' calculations based on data from the Early Childhood Longitudinal Study—Kindergarten cohort. Bars show differences on an SAT-type scale between children in the top and bottom 20% of the income distribution in kindergarten and 5th grade.

Note: A positive gap, shown above the bar, indicates that richer students scored higher than poorer students on this measure (as in the case of reading achievement and school engagement). A negative gap, shown below the bar, indicates that poorer students scored higher than richer students on this measure (as in the case of antisocial behavior and mental health problems).

The study first assessed the children shortly after they began kindergarten, providing a picture of their skills at the starting line of their formal schooling. It shows that children from families in the top 20 percent of the income distribution already outscore children from the bottom 20 percent by 106 points in early literacy. This difference is nearly twice the size of the gap between the average reading skills of white and both black and Hispanic children at that age, and nearly equal to the amount that the typical child learns during kindergarten. Moreover, the reading gap was even larger when the same children were tested in fifth grade. Gaps in mathematics achievement are also substantial.[2]

Children are more successful in school when they are able to pay attention, when they get along with peers and teachers, and when they are not preoccupied or depressed because of troubles at home. Using the same SAT-type metric as for reading scores, figure 3.1 shows that, according to teachers, children from more affluent families are more engaged than their low-income peers. Also, children from low-income families are more likely to engage in antisocial behavior and to have mental health problems. These differences are smaller than the differences in reading skills. None of these advantages for high-income children shrinks over the course of elementary school, nor do they decline as children move to high school. Indeed, another national data set focusing on eighth graders in 1988 shows that 95 percent of students from families in the top quarter of the income distribution graduated from high school, as compared with only 64 percent of those from the bottom quarter.[3] As we saw in chapter 2, the income-based gap in college graduation rates is even larger and has grown sharply over the last three decades.

Why might growing gaps in family income cause an increasing gap between the school success of low-income and higher-income children? According to economic theory, families with higher incomes are better able to purchase or produce important "inputs" into their young children's development—for example, nutritious meals, enriched home learning environments and child-care settings outside the home, and safe and stimulating neighborhood environments.[4] Alternatively, psychologists and sociologists focus on how economic disadvantage impairs the quality of family relationships.[5] We consider each of these explanations in turn.

ENRICHMENT EXPENDITURES

Increasing income inequality contributes to the growth in achievement gaps, in part because income enables parents to promote learning opportunities and avoid some of the myriad risks to the healthy development of their children.[6] Garrett Tallinger is the pseudonym given by Lareau to a white fourth grader living with his well-to-do parents and two brothers in a four-bedroom "classic home in the suburbs." Like Alexander at that age, Garrett is tall and thin, and while his personality is more introverted than Alexander's, his competitiveness is on display during his frequent sports activities. Tracking the details of Garrett's life for several weeks, Lareau's fieldworkers observed him as he played baseball and soccer, practiced with his swim team, and took piano and saxophone lessons. All but the saxophone were extracurricular activities. They consumed an inordinate amount of the family's weekday and weekend time, and also cost a lot of money: "Soccer costs $15 per month, but there are additional, larger expenses periodically. The . . . soccer team's new warm-up suits, socks and shirts cost the Tallingers $100. Piano runs $23 per weekly lesson per child. Tennis clinic is $50; winter basketball $30. It costs the family money to drive to out-of-state tournaments and stay overnight. Fees for Garrett's summer camps have varied; some have cost $200 per week . . . [Mrs. Tallinger] reported expenditures for Garrett alone as exceeding $4,000 per year, a figure that other middle-class families also report."[7]

These kinds of expenses were not unusual for the upper-middle-class families in Lareau's study. All could easily afford comfortable and reliable cars to transport their children from activity to activity. All lived in spacious houses in quiet, relatively crime-free neighborhoods.

Circumstances were very different for the working-class and welfare-recipient families. We have already seen the financial constraints that Anthony Mears's family labored under. His family did not have a reliable car and his mother worried about crime in the neighborhood.

Harold McAlister is another of the children described in Lareau's book. His family's income is even lower than Anthony's. When observed in fourth grade, Harold, who is African American, has a stocky build and loves to play basketball and football with his friends whenever he can. He is living with his family in a two-story, four-bedroom brick public housing unit in an all-black urban neighborhood. The apartment is home to Harold's mother, her common-law husband, two sisters, an older brother and, from time to time, some cousins. Harold's father, who works as a car mechanic and lives nearby, never married his mother, but his regular visits to the family keep him connected with Harold.

Harold's mother is as passionate as Garrett's parents about providing what it takes for her children to be successful and happy, but she sees her role as providing food, "clothing and shelter, teaching the difference between right and wrong, and providing comfort."[8] In contrast to Garrett, Harold—like Anthony—is free to play with the many children in the neighborhood, and is not expected to ask permission.

Permission *is* needed if Harold or his sister wants something to eat, because food is always in short supply: "One Friday night, for instance, the two pizzas in the oven must be divided among [six family members]. When Harold asks for a second piece of pizza, he is redirected to drink soda. Another night, each child has one meatball, canned yams, and canned spinach for dinner. There is not enough for second helpings." Even more revealing is Harold's younger sister's response when asked what she would do if she had a million dollars: "Oh boy! I'd buy my brother, my sister, my uncle, my aunt, my nieces, and my nephews, and my grand-pop, and my grandmom, and my mom, and my dad, and my friends, not my friends, but mostly my best friend—I'd buy them all clothes . . . and sneakers . . . and I'd buy my mom some food, and I'd get my brothers and my sisters gifts for their birthdays."[9]

This level of deprivation can harm children in many ways.[10] Poor nutrition and inadequate health care have long-term effects on children's intellectual development. Exposure to lead paint affects children's nervous systems, resulting in hyperactivity and irritability, with long-term consequences for both intellectual and emotional development. Exposure to violence results in an inability to stay focused on the task at hand. In other words, poverty creates deficits in children that are long-lasting and very difficult to overcome. Moreover, as we explain in the next chapter, children with cognitive and behavior problems in school can consume a disproportionate share of classroom time and school resources and in so doing reduce their classmates' learning.

More income enables families to purchase better housing in better neighborhoods and thereby reduce their children's exposure to neighborhood violence and toxins such as lead and airborne pollutants, while increasing access to parks, playgrounds, better schools, and health care. National consumer expenditure data provide a systematic look at spending differences between high- and low-income families.[11] High-income families report spending twice as much on food and four times as much on housing and clothing as low-income families. Schooling outcomes are likely to be affected most by "child enrichment" expenditures—extracurricular activities like the sports Garrett played, high-quality child care for preschoolers, home-learning materials, and Alexander's private schooling. Anthony's family scraped together enough money to pay his school tuition in his senior year, but Harold's family was having trouble putting enough food on the table.

Forty years ago, low-income families spent about $880 (in 2012 dollars) on child enrichment expenditures, while higher-income families spent more than $3,700, already a substantial difference (figure 3.2).[12] By 2005–2006, low-income families had increased their expenditures to about $1,400, but high-income families had increased theirs much more, to more than $9,300 per child. The differences in spending between the two groups had almost tripled in the intervening years. Activities such as music lessons, travel, and summer camps accounted for the largest difference.[13]

STRESS AND MENTAL HEALTH

Another factor that affects school achievement is the quality of family relationships. When families are free from persistent strain, relationships are easier and less fraught with tension.[14] When parent-child relationships are warm, children respond well. When children respond well, harsh parenting practices are less common. Research has shown that parenting tends to differ depending on a family's position on the income spectrum.[15]

Figure 3.2   Family enrichment expenditures on children by income level

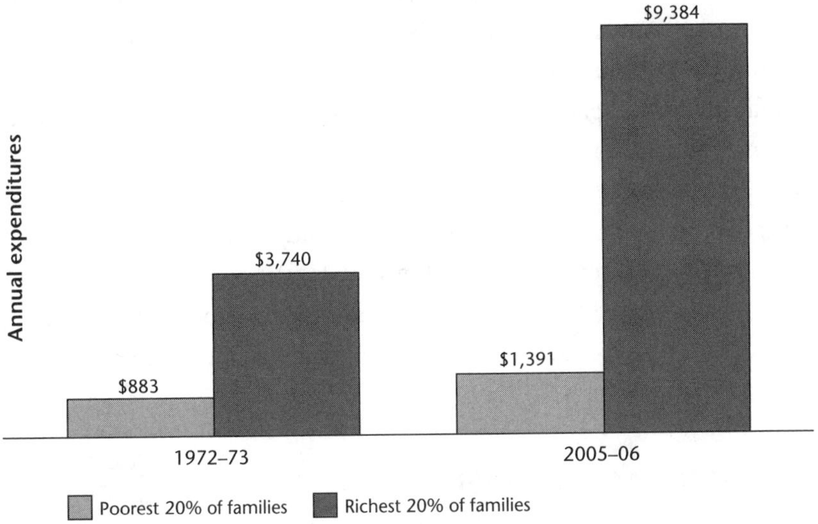

Source: Authors' calculations based on data from the Consumer Expenditure Surveys. Amounts are in 2012$.

Depression and other forms of psychological distress can profoundly affect parents' interactions with their children.[16] It is difficult to determine the extent to which poverty causes poor mental health and harsh parenting, since so many factors are associated with low family incomes. Absent fathers, past or present substance abuse, a parent's lack of education, and early childbearing are all factors that can influence parental mental health and childrearing. However, two recent studies have been able to disentangle some of the causes and effects to show the role of income in mental health, work-family balance, and children's school success. One study found that mothers' reports of their mental health were more positive after the Earned Income Tax Credit (EITC) program increased its payments to working families.[17] This suggests that the strain of low income takes a toll on maternal mental health. Analyzing data from blood samples, the researchers also found lower levels of biomarkers for maternal stress after the EITC expansions.

A second promising piece of evidence has emerged from a study of the New Hope work-support program, which operated in two poor neighborhoods in Milwaukee in the late 1990s. The objective of this intervention was to help low-income families balance the stressful demands of work and family. Participating adults were offered a menu of benefits—a cash earnings supplement, child care and health care subsidies, temporary community service jobs—provided that the families maintained at least a thirty-hour work week. Results from a random-assignment evaluation showed that children, especially boys, of families participating in New Hope demonstrated higher school achievement and better behavior than their control group counterparts. (This program is described in greater detail in chapter 8.)

ACADEMIC ACHIEVEMENT

Enrichment expenditures and improved mental health, lower stress, and more "room for error" are some of the potential reasons that increased income might be associated with better school progress among lower-income children. What do all of these possible influences add up to? Two experimental studies involving three sites examined the overall impacts on children of income supplements that boosted family income by as much as 50 percent. In two of the three sites, the researchers found that children in families randomly assigned to receive an income supplement did significantly better with respect to early academic achievement and school attendance than children in families that received no supplement.[18]

Similar results showed up in experimental welfare reform studies from the 1990s.[19] Income-boosting programs produced improvements in children's academic achievement in preschool and elementary school, while programs that only increased employment did not. A $3,000 increase in annual family income raised young children's achievement test scores by the equivalent of about 20 SAT points, on average—not a huge amount, but equal to about two-thirds of the growth in the test-score gap between richer and poorer children in the past three decades.[20]

Thus the strongest research evidence appears to indicate that money matters, in a variety of ways, for children's long-term success in school.[21]

The circumstances in which Anthony and Harold grew up, shaped in large part by their families' lower incomes, have left a mark. While some children have always enjoyed greater benefits and advantages than others, the income gap has widened dramatically over the past four decades.

FAMILY STRUCTURE AND PARENTAL EDUCATION

While income inequality has played a role in widening the educational divide, it is far from the only factor influencing life chances and academic success. Neither Anthony nor Harold had a father living with him most of the time, although both retained connections with their fathers. Single-parent family structures have become the norm for low-income children but are still quite rare among children in high-income families.[22] Growing up in a single-parent family appears to have particularly detrimental consequences for male children, in part because they receive less attention than daughters and in part because their behavior is especially sensitive to levels of attention and warmth.[23]

Parental education levels probably matter even more than family structure and income.[24] Alexander's and Garrett's parents had a keen sense of what it would take for their sons to gain admission to a top university; for example, Alexander's mother helped him secure a summer internship in a medical office. None of Anthony's or Harold's parents had any experience with a four-year college. In her conversations with Lareau, Harold's mother revealed that she was not acquainted with anyone who was a teacher, reading specialist, family counselor, psychologist, doctor, or lawyer.

These kinds of differences affect children's daily experiences and ultimately their educational outcomes. Even if the income gap were to narrow, some of these other differences would remain and continue to influence children's educational outcomes. In the 1970s, Betty Hart and Todd Risley discovered an important source of a literacy gap among kindergarteners.[25] The researchers recruited forty-four families with children who had just celebrated their first birthdays. Hart and Risley made an effort to recruit families from all socioeconomic strata—professional, working class, and welfare recipients—all of which were residentially stable and relatively free of dysfunction. For the next two years, team members paid monthly visits to the families' homes and tape-recorded and then transcribed every word spoken by the child and parents. Next, they looked at the number and complexity of the words, parts of speech, clauses, verb tenses, and declarative sentences, and determined whether a sentence was an affirmative response to something a child had said. Neither Hart nor Risley took a single day of vacation for three years!

The study generated the often-cited finding that over a year's time, professional parents utter an average of eleven million words to their toddlers. The corresponding figures for working-class and welfare families were six and three million, respectively. There was a long list of class-related language differences.[26] And some of these language differences were associated with reading achievement when the children were in fourth grade. National data later confirmed some of the differences identified by Hart and Risley. For example, while 72 percent of middle-class children start school knowing their letters, this is true of only 19 percent of poor children. And three times as many middle-class as poor children know beginning word sounds.[27]

The Hart and Risley study is a sobering reminder that it takes more than money to promote young children's development.[28] Parents from higher-income families appear to offer their children language advantages that would persist even if their annual incomes rose or fell by $10,000 or even $20,000. Research has shown that maternal education and IQ levels, not family income, are most closely associated with parental use of language.[29] So while money matters, other family factors do too.

Lareau's detailed look at the lives of the children in her study revealed other striking differences between high- and low-income families, including the degree to which middle-class parents "managed" their children's lives, while working-class and poor parents left children alone to play and otherwise organize their activities.

> In the middle class, life was hectic. Parents were racing from activity to activity. In families with more than one child, parents often juggled conflicts between children's activities . . . Because there were so many activities, and because they were accorded so much importance, children's activities determined the schedule for the entire family . . . [In contrast], the limited economic resources available to working-class and poor families make

getting children fed, clothed, sheltered and transported time-consuming, arduous labor. Parents tend to direct their efforts toward keeping children safe, enforcing discipline, and, when they deem it necessary, regulating their behavior in specific areas. . . Thus, whereas middle-class children are often treated as a project to be developed, working-class and poor children are given boundaries for their behavior and then allowed to grow.[30]

We may not be able to untangle the precise effects of all these family-related factors—language use, parental management strategies, and family stress—on the disparities in children's school readiness and success that have emerged over the past several decades. But the evidence linking income to children's school achievement that we have reviewed suggests that the sharp increase in income differences since the 1970s and the concomitant gap in children's school success by income is hardly coincidental. Moreover, as states have raised academic standards—a topic we address in the next chapter—the differential impact of income on family life may mean more than it did in the past.

America has long depended on its schools to help level the playing field for children who are disadvantaged by early family conditions. Horace Mann, an early advocate of public education in the United States, argued that schools could help to "equalize the conditions of men." Current data show that less advntaged children start school well behind their more fortunate peers. The gaps in academic performance and behavior between high- and low-income children do not decrease between kindergarten and high school, and they are larger now than at any point in the last forty years. Part of the reason is that school quality itself has been affected by rising income inequality. How and why this should be so is the subject of the next chapter.

4

Challenges in the Classroom

IN THE LATE 1980s, the Massachusetts town of Holyoke was struggling with a decades-long decline in its industrial base. Some 150 years earlier, its strategic location on the Connecticut River had made it a destination for shipping from Long Island Sound and a home to mills that produced more paper than any other place in the world; this continued until the middle of the twentieth century. The first and largest group of immigrants to Holyoke was Irish. In fact, Holyoke still hosts the second largest St. Patrick's Day parade in the nation, ranking only behind New York City's. Eventually, though, Irish workers were replaced by French-Canadians and then immigrants from an assortment of Eastern European countries. In the late 1950s, a wave of Puerto Ricans began to arrive in Holyoke.

Holyoke is close enough to Springfield, Massachusetts, to be considered part of the greater Springfield metropolitan area—the second largest in Massachusetts. By 1990, though, the city's population had fallen by a third from its peak seventy years before. And while the Holyoke school district still included some middle-class areas like the Highlands, the heart of the city contained more than a few blighted neighborhoods. The district's policy was to balance the economic and ethnic composition of its schools; for Kelly Elementary School in the late 1980s, a typical year's enrollment was 314 Hispanic (mostly Puerto Rican) children, 265 whites, 30 blacks, and 11 Asians.

Among Schoolchildren, by Tracy Kidder, chronicles the school year of Christine Zajac, one of Kelly's fifth-grade teachers, during this same period.[1]

Kidder observed Zajac's classroom, school, and community, and talked with a number of her students' parents, but his account concentrates on Zajac and the fifth graders themselves. With fourteen years of teaching experience to draw on, Chris Zajac devoted considerable teaching skills and energy to her students over the course of the school year.

While no single school can possibly typify the broad range of struggling schools in our country, Kelly School in the late 1980s shared many features common to such schools today. Its students spanned the spectrum from above to far below grade level in their academic skills and, depending on the day and the student, from cooperative to defiant and from attentive to disengaged in their behavior. Some came from profoundly poor and dysfunctional single-parent families, while others lived with two middle-class parents in quiet Holyoke neighborhoods. And while the better students tended to come from the more affluent families, the correlation was far from perfect; Zajac's highest-achieving student lived in one of Holyoke's poorest neighborhoods. More than anything, Zajac tried to nurture the academic skills of the children whose lives had dealt them difficult hands and whose trajectories were often leading to dropout and early parenthood.

In many ways, Zajac exemplifies the elementary school teachers that our nation has relied on to educate many generations of students. She grew up in Holyoke, graduated from one of the state's public colleges, and teaches close to her childhood home. She always liked to read, but struggled in math. Zajac has strong classroom management skills, which are highly valued by the school principal and her students' parents. Zajac especially likes to teach reading and writing and is quite successful at improving her students' skills in these areas. She is less comfortable teaching mathematics; aware of her limitations in this area, she is a bit frustrated that no useful help is available. Zajac dislikes teaching science, primarily because she knows little about it. So she lets creative writing run over into the time for teaching science, and on about one day in ten she cancels science instruction entirely.

Zajac and her colleagues know that many of the students at their school fail to master important skills. But since most of the teachers are already working as hard as they can, they don't see how they can improve this situation. Working with colleagues to improve instruction is not part of the teachers' job description. The school schedule sets aside no time for collaboration within grade-level teams, and Zajac has not seen most of her colleagues teach. The school principal had observed one of Zajac's lessons in the previous year, and commented only that she was doing a good job. Kidder writes, "Chris had nearly absolute autonomy inside her room. In that narrow, complicated place, she was the only arbiter of her own conduct. Sometimes she felt very lonely. 'The worst about it,' she once said, 'is you don't even know if you're doing something wrong.'"[2]

Teachers like Chris Zajac and school systems like Holyoke's served the country well for the first three-quarters of the twentieth century.[3] Most students learned to read well enough to follow directions and learned enough mathematics to balance checkbooks. These skills enabled most high school graduates to enjoy a standard of living higher than that of their parents.

The nation's education problem today is not that schools have become less effective in imparting basic skills to students from low-income families. Indeed, evidence from the National Assessment of Educational Progress (NAEP), often called "The Nation's Report Card," shows that today low-income students' mastery of basic skills, particularly math, is somewhat superior to that of their counterparts forty years ago.[4] The problem is that the skills of low-income students have kept pace neither with the skills of children in higher-income families, nor with the skills demanded by many jobs paying middle-class wages.

Using methods very similar to the ones their own teachers used, Zajac and her fellow teachers work hard, teaching most of their students the skills they themselves learned in school. But while these skills may still lead to high school diplomas, those diplomas no longer produce earnings that enable their recipients to share in the fruits of America's economic growth.

RISING ACADEMIC STANDARDS

As we explained in chapter 2, changes in the American economy over the last thirty years have dramatically reduced the number of jobs that pay a middle-class wage for such routine tasks as filing, typing, and assembly-line work. Increasingly, jobs that pay well require employees to be able to solve unexpected problems, often while working in groups, and to communicate effectively, both orally and in writing. These shifts in labor force demands have in turn put new and increasingly stringent demands on schools.

In the early 1980s, in response to concerns that an inadequately skilled labor force had contributed to a decade of slow economic growth, then–U.S. Secretary of Education T. H. Bell appointed a blue-ribbon commission to examine American education. The group's highly publicized 1983 report, *A Nation at Risk*, concluded that "the educational foundations of our society are presently being eroded by a rising tide of mediocrity that threatens our very future as a Nation and a people."[5] Among other things, the Commission recommended that before receiving a high school diploma, students should be required to complete four years of English and three years of mathematics, science, and social studies. In the years following publication of the report, many states responded by increasing course requirements for high school graduation.

By the early 1990s, attempts to improve public education had moved toward a standards-based educational reform agenda. While details vary greatly from state to state, standards-based educational reforms typically include content standards that specify what students should know and be able to do at each grade level, assessments that measure the extent to which students have met the standards, and incentives for students and educators. Because of the standards-based educational reform movement, by the 2009–2010 school year 75 percent of all public high school students and 83 percent of all students of color in the United States were required to pass at least one exit examination in order to obtain a high school diploma.[6]

Standards-based educational reforms meant that students at each grade level were expected to master more complex skills than their predecessors. For example, compare the two test items in figure 4.1. The first column is a typical item from the Basic Skills test that Massachusetts public school sixth graders took in the early 1980s.[7] The second column is a question taken from the sixth-grade mathematics test that all Massachusetts public school students took in 2011.[8]

Figure 4.1   Questions reflecting sixth-grade math standards

Early 1980s	2011

Early 1980s

Carol can ride her bike 10 miles per hour. If Carol rides her bike to the store, how long will it take?

To solve this problem, you would need to know:

A. How far it is to the store.

B. What kind of bike Carol has.

C. What time Carol will leave.

D. How much Carol has to spend.

2011

Question 17 is an open-response question.

- *BE SURE TO ANSWER AND LABEL ALL PARTS OF THE QUESTION.*
- *Show all your work (diagrams, tables, or computations) in your Student Answer Booklet.*
- *If you do the work in your head, explain in writing how you did the work.*

Write your answer to question 17 in the space provided in your Student Answer Booklet.

Paige, Rosie, and Cheryl **each** spent exactly $9.00 at the same snack bar.

- Paige bought 3 bags of peanuts.
- Rosie bought 2 bags of peanuts and 2 pretzels.
- Cheryl bought 1 bag of peanuts, 1 pretzel, and 1 milk shake.

e. What is the cost, in dollars, of 1 bag of peanuts? Show or explain how you got your answer.

f. What is the cost, in dollars, of 1 pretzel? Show or explain how you got your answer.

g. What is the total number of pretzels that can be bought for the cost of 1 milk shake? Show or explain how you got your answer.

The introduction of the Common Core State Standards promises to raise the bar even higher, and to direct educators' efforts in more productive ways. For reasons we will discuss in chapter 9, we believe this initiative has promise, even as it poses significant challenges to teachers' capabilities.

Requiring students to master more sophisticated skills at each grade level makes sense, given that workers today need more advanced skills to earn a middle-class living than in the past. Where higher standards have resulted in better education, children from all income groups have benefited.[9] However, in many states, increases in high school graduation requirements have not been accompanied by significant improvements in the quality of education children receive, especially those attending high-poverty schools. While poor education has always hampered life chances for low-income children, the negative effects are even greater when failure to pass exit examinations prevents students from obtaining a high school diploma.[10] Thus, more stringent high school graduation standards, which have the potential to benefit children from both affluent and low-income families, have inadvertently exacerbated the consequences of differences in schooling quality and the effects of growing income inequality on the life chances of children growing up in low-income families.

The key challenge is to ensure that instruction in American classrooms is up to the task of providing all American children with the education they will need to meet higher academic standards. But the path to better instruction is filled with obstacles. Consider reading instruction. Historically, the dominant approach has been whole-class instruction using textbooks.[11] This provided students with the reading skills needed to follow directions, which was adequate in an economy in which this was the only literacy requirement in a great many jobs. However, as explained in chapter 2, changes in the economy have eliminated many of these kinds of jobs. Today, the literacy requirements in most jobs paying decent wages include the ability to conduct an Internet search efficiently and to judge what small portion of the thousands of responses to any query provides useful information. They also include the ability to make sense of the new information constantly encountered as a person faces new problems. The traditional approach to teaching reading leaves a great many students without these skills.

Partly in response to the mismatch between traditional instructional methods and new academic standards, many schools and school districts have adopted new curricula that provide daily opportunities for group work and initiative as well as direct teacher-led instruction in critical skills. An example in the primary grades is balanced literacy, which integrates explicit instruction in letter-sound relationships and spelling patterns with the reading of age- and skill-level-appropriate texts and small-group activities such as reading and writing workshops.[12]

When properly implemented, curricula like balanced literacy are powerful strategies for enabling children to acquire the skills and motivation to read challenging texts and to write effectively. However, they are difficult to implement, not least because they are very different from the way teachers themselves were taught. Some teachers worry that if they abandon the teaching strategies they are comfortable with, their students will suffer; others fear losing control of the class. Moreover, these approaches require excellent classroom management skills because children are working in many different groups at the same time. Finally, it takes a great deal of time to set up multiple activity centers each day. Because of these challenges, new curricula like balanced literacy are often not implemented appropriately, and children lose out. As we explain below, this is especially likely to happen in schools serving high concentrations of children from low-income families, due to patterns of classroom dynamics that typically arise when schools are segregated by income.

INCREASING RESIDENTIAL ISOLATION

America's growing income inequality has greatly complicated the task of providing high-quality schooling to low-income children, not least because of the changing residential patterns of high- and low-income families. A number of studies have shown that growing income inequality has led to increases in the residential isolation of families at both ends of the income spectrum. During the thirty-year period between 1970 and 2000, high-income families became increasingly likely to live in neighborhoods with other high-income families. Low-income families became even more isolated.[13] Remarkably, this increased residential segregation by income occurred just as race-based residential segregation was declining.[14]

Because children usually attend schools in the neighborhoods where they live, the gap between the average parental incomes in the schools attended by high- and low-income children has increased. A national study found that in the case of high school students, the gap in classmates' average family income (adjusted for inflation) between the top and bottom of the income distribution jumped by 50 percent between 1972 and 2002.[15]

As high-income and low-income students are increasingly concentrated in separate schools, income-based achievement differences are exacerbated in a number of ways. First, students' learning is affected by the achievement and behavior of their classmates. Because achievement levels tend to be lower and problem behavior more widespread among low-income students, increasing the concentration of poor students in particular schools reduces overall academic achievement in these schools. Second, we know that low-income families are much more likely than high-income families to move during the course of a year and that the achievement of students who change schools during the school year is diminished by the transition, as is the achievement of their new classmates. Third, patterns of immigration compound the challenges because low-income immigrants of color tend to settle in neighborhoods served by the same public schools that low-income native-born students of color attend. Finally, it is difficult to build strong, stable teaching staffs in schools serving large numbers of low-income students because of the difficult working conditions typical of these schools. Increasing the concentration of low-income children in particular schools exacerbates this problem. We consider each of these problems in turn: peer effects, residential mobility, immigration, and teacher quality.

Achievement and Behavior of Peers

While no one has compiled national data on the changes that have taken place since the 1970s in the myriad dimensions of peer achievement and behavior, we know how peer characteristics differ in the kinds of schools attended by high- and low-income students today. As shown in figure 4.2, students in high-poverty schools are nearly four times as likely as students in low-poverty schools to have achievement problems.[16] Teacher ratings of students' behavior problems show similar—although not as extreme—patterns. Increasing concentrations of low-achieving and misbehaving students can have serious implications for the learning that takes place in classrooms.

As Tracy Kidder notes, Chris Zajac was keenly aware of the effects students had on one another. On the first day of school, Zajac let her students choose their desks within a large square arrangement. On the second day, she made some strategic adjustments that were designed to help struggling students and avoid some of the negative peer influences she had come to fear over the years:

Figure 4.2 Peer composition of students in schools with low and high concentrations of poor students

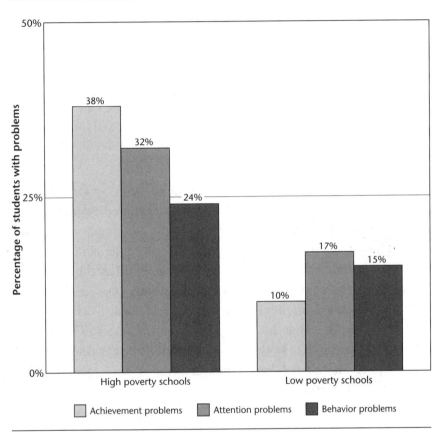

Source: Duncan and Magnuson in Duncan, Greg J., and Richard J. Murnane, eds. Appendix Table 3.A8, "School-level Concentrations of Kindergarten Achievement, Attention, and Behavior Problems." In *Whither Opportunity*. © 2011 Russell Sage Foundation, 112 East 64th Street, New York, NY 10065. Reprinted with permission. https://www.russellsage.org/sites/all/files/duncan_murnane_online_appendix.pdf.

Note: "Low poverty" and "high poverty" are defined as less than 5% and more than 50% of students receiving free or reduced-price lunch, respectively.

She put four desks in the middle of the square, so that each of those four had space between it and any other desk. These were Chris's "middle-person desks," where it was especially hard to hide . . .

She had caught Courtney not paying attention several times yesterday. Courtney was small and doll-like, with a mobile, rubbery face . . . "If school doesn't become important to her, and she doesn't do better at it, she'll have a boyfriend at fourteen and a baby at sixteen." Courtney got a middle-person spot . . .

She sent handsome, enthusiastic Felipe to a spot between Margaret and Alice. Felipe seemed to be very talkative and excitable. He was probably used to being the center of attention. Chris guessed, "He's easily influenced by the people around him. If he sits between twits, he'll be a twit." Placed between two obviously well-mannered children, Felipe might be an asset . . .

Several children seemed quick academically, especially Alice and Judith, a Puerto Rican girl with long, dark, curly hair and penetrating eyes . . . Chris moved Judith next to Alice. "Judith's exceptional, and I want Alice to get to know an Hispanic kid who's at her level." Maybe Judith and Alice would become friends.[17]

Throughout the year, Zajac tracked the children in her class, both as she taught them and as they interacted on the playground. Several months into the school year, Judith had shown herself to be a truly outstanding student. Perhaps it was because her father had filled her childhood with stories, but perhaps also because she had long served as the interpreter for her Spanish-speaking parents as they dealt with stores, social service agencies, and other community institutions. Still, Zajac worried that Judith might not be able to break free from the influences of her impoverished upbringing. Her world was circumscribed by her neighborhood, and Judith and her parents had never even heard of nearby Smith, Mount Holyoke, or Amherst College.

From her classroom window in the crisp, dying days of fall, Chris would watch her students at recess on the playground below . . . Chris had begun to see Judith hanging around in a group that included a very tough thirteen-year-old fifth grader from another homeroom, a pretty girl with a dirty neck, who leered at handsome boys and was often seen sitting on the bad-boy chairs outside Al's [the principal's] office. Then one day Chris saw that girl stuff some clothes under her coat at recess and promenade around, pantomiming pregnancy, while a small group of girls, which included Judith, watched. It looked as though Judith was laughing.[18]

Zajac did what she could to combat these developments. At her next conference with Judith's parents, with Judith acting as interpreter, she made sure that the parents understood how smart their daughter was and that she would surely qualify for a college scholarship if she continued to work hard in school. And at school, Zajac arranged for Judith to spend time working in the school library while classroom time was devoted to the lower-achieving students.

Perhaps the most harmful peer effects are generated by students whose behavior disrupts the learning environment for their classmates. Over the years, Zajac had developed an array of strategies for keeping things in check. As one of her students was overheard to comment, "She knows every trick in the book." Although short in stature, Zajac was an energetic and arresting presence in the classroom. Her voice commanded attention, as did her frequent and theatrical gestures. But these features mattered much less than more subtle skills.

> Classroom management, as Mrs. Zajac practiced it, required an enlarge-ment of the senses . . . Chris could tell, without seeing, not only that a child was running on the stairs but also that the footfalls belonged to Clarence, and she could turn her attention to curing one child's confusion and still know that Clarence was whispering threats to Arabella. She was always scanning the room with her eyes without moving her head, seeing without being seen . . . [T]here had developed in Chris a sense not easily accounted for—like a hunter's knack for spotting a piece of furry ear and inferring a deer standing in the thicket—so that, for example, she could sit at the slide projector, pausing in a filmstrip to lecture the class on the Iroquois, and know that, behind her, Robert wasn't paying attention. In fact, Robert was playing baton with his pencil, noiselessly flipping it in the air. Chris didn't stop talking to the class or even turn around. Extending her left hand back toward Robert, she snapped her fingers once. Robert stopped flipping his pencil and, as usual, blushed.[19]

For the first several months of most school years, Zajac's classroom served as a training ground for a student teacher from a local state college. She was well aware that the ability to control a classroom is the most dif-ficult skill for novice teachers to master. As part of her training, this year's student teacher would be left alone to teach occasional lessons. Sometimes these went well; on other occasions, the behavior of students would spin out of control and pandemonium would quickly ensue.

Classroom management looms large in the minds of principals as they make their hiring decisions, particularly in poor schools. A study of prin-cipals in the Chicago public school system found that in schools with low concentrations of poor students, the principal rated "the candidate's enthusiasm for teaching" well above all other criteria, while principals of schools serving many poor students put "the candidate's classroom management skills" on top.[20] Here is how one principal of a struggling school put it:

> First of all I'm looking for someone who knows how to manage a classroom, because many of the new hires that I have hired over the last 10 years, they're good academically, some of them have been . . . 4.0 and so forth, but when it comes to teaching, they cannot teach because they don't have the skills to deal with classroom management, and that's key. And our kids—I'm just coming from a classroom now, someone I just hired. They are afraid to tell children to sit and learn. Those same set[s] of children can go to the next classroom and you won't even know it's an issue.[21]

When misbehavior did occur, Zajac had a variety of threats and incentives that she could employ to bring the wayward student into line. She rarely sent students to the principal's office, knowing that the student would lose valuable learning time. After all, even Clarence, her most problematic student, was, at times, sweet and capable of writing poems or little essays that reflected academic skills worth nurturing. In the end, though, Clarence's fighting and other unacceptable behavior grew so disruptive that, against Zajac's recommendation, the school decided to transfer him to a special school for children with severe behavior problems. Within a few weeks, Zajac

> told herself that she was witnessing real progress that wouldn't have been possible with Clarence in the room . . . She missed him sometimes, but in the midst of missing him she recalled sitting with him at her table, trying to get him to write a story, his face growing stonier the harder she tried. She'd remember wasting half of the hour of creative writing trying to get him to work, and wasting most of the next half hour trying to regain her composure. She would remember coming back from lunch to find Arabella sobbing, and would remember knowing at that instant that she'd have to lecture Clarence again and that doing so would mean he'd put on the stony face and cause more trouble in the room the next time she turned her back. She'd remember thinking, "all I want to do is teach. I want a quiet afternoon so I can teach."[22]

It is difficult to assess systematically the impact of one student's misbehavior on the achievement of other students, since parents and schools often play a role in determining which students end up with which teachers. If teachers who are highly skilled at managing problem behavior in their classrooms tend to be assigned the most difficult students, then student learning may occur even in the presence of a problematic classmate. At the other extreme, if novice teachers are assigned to classes with children who have behavior problems, then the peer effects of misbehavior might appear much larger than they would be with a more typical teacher.

Researchers have tried to get around this teacher-student assignment problem in a number of ways. One well-designed study found that the presence in a classroom of children from homes in which domestic violence had taken place reduced the academic achievement of their classmates. This was an especially common occurrence in schools serving high concentrations of children from low-income families.[23] A second found gains in classmate achievement after children with attention problems were diagnosed and (presumably) treated.[24]

In short, a considerable body of research has confirmed the intuition about peer effects that Chris Zajac quickly developed after she began teaching. And since increasing the concentration of low-income students in particular schools has almost certainly increased the prevalence of behavior problems in those schools, we expect that a significant portion of the increasing achievement gap between affluent and low-income students can be attributed to these kinds of peer effects.

Mobility

Student mobility poses another threat to achievement. When teachers are faced with a steady stream of new students over the course of the school year, they must juggle the tasks of assessing the new students' skills and helping them to understand and abide by classroom behavioral norms while keeping the rest of the students moving through the curriculum. Integrating new students is particularly time-consuming and challenging when students are working at multiple activity centers in small groups. Thus, pedagogies that offer great potential to help children learn to work

productively in groups and communicate effectively are especially difficult to implement in classrooms with transient students.

We have long known that low-income families are more residentially
mobile than higher-income families; recent census data show that more
than twice as many low-income as high-income households move in any
given year.[25] A Chicago-based study confirms that as a result of school
sorting by socioeconomic status, children from low-income families are
more likely to attend schools with relatively high rates of new students
arriving during the school year.[26] In a typical Chicago elementary school,
about one in ten of the students enrolled at the end of the school year had
arrived after the school year began. In the poorest schools, the fraction
was closer to 20 percent. With average school enrollments of about 800
students, this means that as many as 160 new students arrive during the
school year, about five per classroom.

The Chicago study also found that children attending elementary
schools with high rates of student mobility made less progress in mathematics than children in schools with low student mobility. And the negative effects apply to students who themselves are residentially stable as
well as to those who are not. Although we lack data to track changes in
student turnover in poor and affluent communities over the past thirty
years, it seems reasonable to suspect that the increasing concentration of
low-income students in certain schools has been accompanied by greater
student mobility and negative impacts on achievement.

English Language Learners

Another challenge facing many of the nation's schools is an influx of immigrants, some of whom speak little English. Nationally, the share of students in kindergarten through twelfth grade with a foreign-born parent
tripled from 6 percent in 1970 to 19 percent in 2000. It is estimated that
children of immigrants composed more than one-quarter of the student
population in 2010.[27] Today's immigrants are more likely than immigrants
in the early 1970s to come from high-poverty countries.

A recent study of public schools in New York City found that black and
Hispanic immigrants to New York City are much more likely to be poor

than are white immigrants from Eastern Europe, and they are more likely to attend elementary and middle schools with native-born black and Hispanic students who are also poor.[28] Thus, while immigrants are not segregated from the native-born in New York City schools as a matter of policy, their sorting across neighborhoods contributes to segregation of schools by socioeconomic status and race. In this way, patterns of immigration, residential location, and language problems exacerbate the growing gap in educational outcomes between children from affluent and low-income families.

Teacher Quality

Recent research supports what most parents believe—that some teachers are much more effective than others and that having consistently effective or ineffective teachers makes a big difference in children's chances of success in school and subsequently in the labor force.[29] Research has also shown that while effective teachers come in all sizes and colors, they have in common a deep understanding of the material they teach, the ability to implement curricula well and to manage their classrooms effectively, and a profound belief in their students' potential along with a commitment to their learning.

Teachers do not start out effective. In fact, one of the most consistent patterns in the research evidence is that teachers become more effective during their first years in the classroom.[30] Those who do become effective develop the requisite skills over time, typically with the support of colleagues who help them learn the complex craft of teaching.[31] Unfortunately, many college graduates enter teaching without strong subject knowledge and never learn to become effective teachers. Others enter with strong subject matter knowledge, but do not receive the support they need to acquire the complex pedagogical and classroom management skills that are essential for effective teaching.

Schools serving low-income students are particularly unlikely to attract and retain effective teachers.[32] As a result, these schools are typically staffed by a disproportionate number of novice teachers whose daily work is dominated by classroom management challenges, with relatively little time left for uninterrupted instruction. Professional development aimed at improving the effectiveness of teachers in high-poverty schools is undermined by high teacher turnover. Moreover, teachers in high-poverty schools improve their performance at a slower rate than do teachers in schools serving middle-class children, perhaps as a result of relatively ineffective colleagues and high rates of teacher turnover.[33] In addition, the introduction of school accountability systems may contribute to the stress of teaching in high-poverty schools and to the difficulty these schools experience in attracting effective teachers, since poor student scores jeopardize teachers' job security.[34]

As if these problems were not enough, there are also factors beyond the classroom that contribute to the difficulty high-poverty schools experience in building strong teaching staffs. A lack of physical safety around some high-poverty schools deters some strong applicants from accepting teaching positions.[35] And the locational preferences of teachers often matter as well. High-poverty schools are typically located in high-poverty neighborhoods where teachers are reluctant to live. Particularly as they begin families of their own, teachers want to work close to their homes.[36] So they seek jobs in or near middle-class neighborhoods. The net effect is that children in a great many high-poverty schools do not receive the high-quality instruction they need to learn critical skills.[37]

In principle, it should be possible to attract effective teachers to schools serving high concentrations of poor children by offering additional pay and better working conditions to compensate for the difficulty of the job. However, conventional practice offers neither of these benefits. Instead, the typical school district salary schedule pays teachers on the basis of their years of experience and academic credentials, not on the basis of their effectiveness or the difficulty of the teaching challenge. And working conditions tend to be particularly difficult in schools serving high concentrations of low-income students.[38] As a result, effective teachers have significant incentives to teach in a middle-class school near their homes rather than in a high-poverty school—where they are especially needed because parents lack the resources to compensate for ineffective teaching.

Rules regarding transfers are yet another problem. While the details vary, most of the contracts negotiated between school districts and teacher unions stipulate that access to open teaching positions is to be based on seniority. Consequently, many teachers in high-poverty schools leave as soon as they have acquired sufficient seniority to obtain a position in a school serving middle-class children. Once again, high-poverty schools are left with a great many novice teachers and high rates of teacher turnover, both of which contribute to low student achievement.

WHAT WILL HELP OUR SCHOOLS SUCCEED?

In recent decades we have learned a great deal about what must happen at school to educate large numbers of low-income children well. In the next three chapters, we describe those lessons as they have played out in educational initiatives that have made a difference in the lives of a considerable number of low-income children. The initiatives differ in some respects, as is only appropriate, since they serve children of different ages with different developmental needs. However, they have two important elements in common. The first is that the schools employing these initiatives have benefited from significant school supports. We use the term *school supports* to refer to the myriad types of resources and expertise high-poverty schools need to achieve sustained success.[39] In one case, the supports come from a school district's Department of Early Childhood, in a second from a charter management organization, and in a third from a combination of community partners and not-for-profit organizations set up to support schools. While the supports depend somewhat on the ages and backgrounds of students, the following are critical common elements:

- Academic standards that provide clear statements about the skills and knowledge that students should master at each grade level
- Assessments that measure students' mastery of the standards well
- Curricula aligned with standards that, if implemented well, enable students to master the standards
- School leaders who know what good instruction looks like and how to create an organization committed to continuous improvement
- Well-educated teachers with deep knowledge of subject matter and how to teach it and who want to work with low-income children
- Teacher access to expertise on a host of topics, including improving instruction, identifying the strengths and weaknesses of individual

students, creating and implementing norms for student behavior, and dealing with students' emotional problems

- Clean, well-maintained physical facilities
- Sufficient resources to implement a schedule that provides time for collaboration, instruction, and remediation, and to provide the special services that emotionally troubled and learning disabled students may need

The second common element is that the schools have faced accountability pressures. One aspect is the need to demonstrate adequate yearly progress on state-mandated tests of students' reading and mathematical skills. However, a more immediate source of accountability pressure in the schools we highlight are cultures in which all teachers are expected to work together to enhance the the development of every child. This combination of consistently strong supports and well-designed accountability— a term we explain in more detail in chapter 9—is essential if high-poverty schools are to be successful in ameliorating the growing disadvantages that children from low-income families in the United States face.

It is important to understand that school improvement strategies require *both* strong school supports and a well-designed accountability system. Accountability in the absence of the school supports necessary to improve instruction and meet the developmental and learning needs of every student leads to an inappropriate focus on test preparation and other dysfunctional responses that do not serve children well.[40] School supports without accountability often do not result in better education because change is difficult. Moving from an organization in which teachers work primarily by themselves in their own closed-door classrooms to an organization in which collaboration is the norm and teachers examine each other's instruction frequently is disconcerting and threatening. Absent pressure to change the way that they work, a great many teachers and administrators continue to work as they have in the past. Doing so will not prepare low-income students to thrive in a rapidly changing economy.

Unfortunately, the combination of consistently strong supports and well-designed accountability is the exception rather than the rule in high-poverty schools. This explains why relatively few low-income children experience the high quality education that the schools described in the following chapters provide.

5

Promising Prekindergarten Programs

IT IS ALTOGETHER FITTING that we start our exploration of promising education policies at the first free public elementary school in North America—Mather Elementary School in Boston's Dorchester neighborhood. It's 10:00 a.m. on an unseasonably warm day in November. Karla Settles, a young African American teacher, finishes reading *The Little Red Hen Makes a Pizza* to the twenty-two African American and Hispanic children sitting on a rug in her classroom. Ms. Settles's four-year-olds comprise one of three prekindergarten (preK) classes at Mather.

The book introduces the children to new words related to food—*mozzarella cheese, mushrooms, anchovies*, and even *delicatessen*. It also describes concepts relevant to mathematical thinking, such as flattening a ball of dough to make a circle and folding it into other shapes. Ms. Settles announces that the class will now be working on activities based on the book. As she calls out letters of the alphabet, the children whose first names begin with each letter move excitedly to the activity area of their choice.

Some children choose a table in the middle of the room, where they use rolling pins to roll out playdough into the shape of the pizza pans. Others choose the cooking corner, where they put plastic versions of vegetables on the pizza dough, as a teacher's aide asks them to name the vegetables.

This helps them place the new vocabulary words in context. Other children move to easels where they use water colors to paint pictures of pizzas loaded with the vegetables they have just learned about. Still others go to the sink at the side of the room to wash the different-shaped pots and pans and pizza-making utensils.

As the children work together at their tasks, Ms. Settles and the teacher's aide move from group to group, asking questions to help the children understand the steps in the pizza-making process and the meanings of the new words in the story. When children want to move to a different activity center, they are expected to ask the children at that center when they will be finished, which reinforces the communication, self-regulation, and negotiation skills that Ms. Settles has been teaching since the first day of school.

The Little Red Hen Makes a Pizza is one module in a rich curriculum that the Boston Public Schools' Department of Early Childhood (DEC) expects all preK teachers in the district to use. So that they can teach the curriculum effectively, DEC provides manuals detailing the range and sequence of topics to be covered in preparing lessons. DEC also offers extensive coaching to the preK teachers, aimed at helping them implement the curriculum well and learn the classroom management skills for keeping groups of four-year-olds productively and happily engaged.

As we will explain in greater detail, the Boston preK program is showing success at preparing children for school and reducing skill and behavior gaps between children in middle-class and low-income families. In this chapter we explore why investments in such programs are critical to improving the life chances of children growing up in low-income families.

THE IMPORTANCE OF EARLY CHILDHOOD INVESTMENTS

Emerging evidence from neuroscience shows that early childhood is a critical period in the development of the brain "architecture" underlying cognitive, social, emotional, and health outcomes.[1] Infants and young children benefit from environments that provide sensitive, responsive caregiving and a variety of language-rich learning opportunities that are tailored to individual children's capabilities and needs. Research on the malleability (plasticity) of cognitive and language abilities finds these skills to be highly responsive to environmental enrichment during the early childhood period.[2]

How might early childhood education programs take advantage of these opportunities, and what kinds of children stand to benefit the most from them? One compelling view centers on the interactive nature of skill-building and investments from families, preschools, and schools.[3] It posits that children's skills developed in earlier stages of childhood bolster the development of skills in later stages. Moreover, a productive synergy exists between the skills children bring into an early education setting and how much they profit from it. These two components combine to produce the hypothesis that "skill begets skill." One implication of this approach is that the children who stand to benefit the most from K–12 schooling are the ones who enter school with a solid set of school readiness skills.

What kinds of skills and behaviors matter the most for school success? Children who enter kindergarten with literacy and numeracy skills, including knowing letters, numbers, shapes, and beginning and ending word sounds, are most likely to be successful students.[4] Also important is a combination of skills involving focusing attention, filtering out distractions, and keeping in mind several pieces of information at the same time. This combination is called "executive functioning" and is viewed as like the job of an air traffic controller.[5] It, too, is broadly predictive of academic achievement, as learning in classroom environments requires self-regulation and concentration.

The Little Red Hen Makes a Pizza module in Ms. Settles's classroom was designed to promote all of these skills. Reading the story stimulates interest in storybooks, introduces vocabulary about food, numbers, and shapes, and reinforces the rewards of paying attention. The many follow-on activities enable children to channel their abundant energy to enjoyable tasks that promote creativity, fine motor skills, turn-taking, and—through the continuing interaction with Ms. Settles and the teacher's aide—comprehension of the vocabulary used in the book. Some educators and parents worry that attempting to build academic skills before kindergarten will mean replacing playtime with flash cards, worksheets, and desk time. Yet in Ms. Settle's classroom, children are having a lot of fun while learning important skills.

Indeed, all of the prekindergarten teachers in Boston integrate playful activities into the school day. Marina Boni, who helps Boston's preK teachers improve their teaching and classroom management, puts it this way: "I'm a huge fan of play, . . . [of] building joyfulness in a climate for learning . . . [T]hree-, four-, five-year-olds—they've got to be happy learners."

Although preK programs like the ones at Mather are a fairly recent development, early childhood education programs have been around for more than half a century, and rigorous evaluations have shown many of them to be effective. Most of the evidence on the long-run consequences of enrolling children in early childhood education programs comes from a handful of programs designed and run by child development experts. Most famous are the Perry Preschool Program and the Abecedarian Project, both of which served several dozen young African American children from low-income families.[6] While the programs differed in some respects (Abecedarian enrolled younger children and worked with them longer than Perry did), both were designed to develop children's language skills and provide the cognitive and socioemotional skills needed to succeed in school. The programs proved successful in improving the lives of participating children. Perry and Abecedarian children were less likely than similar children who did not participate in these programs to be placed in costly special education classes, and they completed more schooling. Longer-term, Perry also enhanced youths' later employment opportunities and reduced their rates of incarceration.

These findings affirm the predictions of neuroscientists regarding the malleability of brain development during the early childhood years by demonstrating the remarkable potential of preschool programs to improve the life chances of children from low-income families. However, these programs were very small and expensive, and the visionary child development experts who founded them monitored their implementation closely. What are the chances that a large school district like Boston's could afford them and implement them at the level of quality their developers insisted upon?

In assessing the effects of the model programs, it is also important to consider the services available to the comparison group. To identify the benefits of Perry and Abecedarian, researchers compared the outcomes of children who won and lost lotteries for admission.[7] When these programs began decades ago, parents of comparison-group children faced much more limited child-care options than they do today.[8] Moreover, the education levels of low-income mothers were much lower then than now, so they probably devoted less time to home enrichment activities. If the experiences of the comparison group failed to enhance school readiness and success, or perhaps even inhibited children's development, then they set a low bar for measuring improvements achieved by Perry and Abecedarian.

A second body of evidence comes from evaluations of Head Start, a national preschool program introduced in 1965 as part of Lyndon Johnson's Great Society initiative.[9] Today, Head Start provides educational, nutritional, health, and social services to more than 900,000 children from low-income families, at an average cost of $9,000 per child.[10] Head Start centers are run by about 1,600 local agencies, all of which have considerable discretion in the design and operation of their programs. As a result, Head Start services vary widely across sites, as do the length of the program and the educational backgrounds and training of Head Start teachers and aides. Head Start centers can choose their curricula, and most lack the resources to ensure that those curricula are implemented successfully.[11]

Evidence on the impacts of Head Start programs is less than clear-cut. Children who attended Head Start centers twenty to twenty-five years ago appear to have done considerably better than their siblings who were not part of the program.[12] However, a more recent and rigorous study found only short-term gains from attending Head Start; almost none of the academic and behavioral gains persisted to the end of first grade.[13] Although Head Start continues to have a strong national constituency, mixed findings on its effectiveness raise the question of whether a more highly structured program implemented by better educated and better trained teachers would yield more favorable results.[14]

States and a number of large urban school districts have introduced preK programs that are quite different from traditional Head Start programs.

Teacher qualification requirements tend to be higher, and there is a stronger emphasis on academic curricula.[15] While costs and quality vary widely across states,[16] a recent evaluation of these kinds of programs in five states found generally positive effects on children's literacy and numeracy skills, although the magnitude of these effects varied.[17] Another study of a high-quality, full-day preK program in Tulsa found quite large positive effects.[18] The program was offered to children from both low- and higher-income families. Although this increased costs, it also increased support for the program. Moreover, developers believe that this mix of children from different backgrounds contributed to the program's success because low-income children were exposed to children with larger vocabularies and other advantages of growing up in more affluent homes.

PRESCHOOL EDUCATION IN THE BOSTON PUBLIC SCHOOLS

The Boston Public Schools (BPS) face the same challenges as other urban districts in the United States. Three-quarters of the 57,000 students attending the district's public schools come from low-income families. Nearly half speak a first language other than English. As four-year-olds, the children from low-income families have academic skills that lag far behind those of the relatively few children from more affluent families who attend BPS schools.[19] These factors pose significant handicaps as low-income children seek to meet academic standards and pass the high school exit examinations that are required for graduation in Massachusetts. The achievement gaps present at age four go a long way in explaining why the on-time high school graduation rate of BPS students from low-income families is 9 percentage points lower than that of non-poor BPS students.[20]

As part of its strategy to close achievement gaps, Boston began to provide full-day preK education programs for four-year-olds with special needs and a modest number of other four-year-olds who won places through a lottery. In the 2004–2005 school year, BPS had thirty-eight classrooms serving 750 four-year-olds. At the urging of Mayor Thomas Menino, BPS almost doubled the number of preK classes in the 2005–2006 school year, enabling it to serve approximately one-quarter of the four-year-olds whose parents applied for admission. As is common in districts that dramatically increase the supply of preschool education, BPS had difficulty finding enough suitable classrooms and trained teachers.

Aware of the need for leadership of its preschool program, Superintendent Thomas Payzant recruited Dr. Jason Sachs to head a newly formed Department of Early Childhood. With a background in research and evaluation and several years of experience in coordinating preschool programs for the Massachusetts State Department of Education, Sachs recognized the importance of program quality. This led him to commission an independent research group, the Wellesley Centers for Women, to conduct an assessment of the quality of Boston's existing preK program. The report, delivered in August 2006, was sobering. As summarized in the *Boston Globe*, "Boston's public preschool and kindergarten programs are hobbled by mediocre instruction, unsanitary classrooms, and dangerous schoolyards, according to a first-ever study of the programs . . . Three-quarters of teachers reported that they lacked classroom materials, including books. In many classrooms, children spent a lot of their day sitting at desks while teachers lectured, a style frowned upon in early childhood education. As a result, half of the teachers missed signs that children were struggling, the study found."[21]

According to Sachs, the *Boston Globe* article could have cost him his job. It did not, he believes, because the district's interim superintendent, Michael Contompasis, explained to the school committee and city council that evidence on quality was a precondition for improving quality. Sachs was able to make the case to the BPS leadership and to outside funders that instead of greatly expanding the number of preK classrooms, the district should slow the rate of expansion and devote significant resources to improving program quality. Only by doing so, he argued, could preK education in Boston contribute meaningfully to closing achievement gaps.

During the next four years, Sachs and his colleagues in the Department of Early Childhood led the effort to improve preK education in Boston by providing teachers and principals with the kinds of educational supports we described in chapter 4. A critical first step was to choose strong curricula for use in all BPS preK classrooms. Only by mandating common curricula could DEC provide the instructional materials, scope and sequencing manuals, and most important, the coaching and professional development teachers would need to provide a consistently high-quality preschool experience for Boston four-year-olds. Moreover, research indicated that consistent implementation of strong reading and mathematics curricula could create positive "spillover" effects on children's emotional development and executive functioning skills. In Sachs' words, "A strong, engaging [academic] curriculum is a compelling way to deal with many social and emotional issues, in part, because the kids are really learning and are deeply engaged in their work . . . Early childhood classrooms are designed to create social interactions and negotiations and to help children make appropriate choices."[22]

After examining curricula already in use in BPS Early Childhood Learning Centers and assessing the evidence on their efficacy, Sachs and his colleagues chose the Opening the World of Learning (OWL) literacy curriculum and the Building Blocks mathematics curriculum. OWL focuses on developing children's early language and literacy skills and includes a social skills component within each study unit. The Building Blocks curriculum develops children's knowledge of simple arithmetic, geometry, measurement, and spatial relationships. The pedagogical approach expands children's language skills by asking them to explain their mathematical reasoning. Strengths of both curricula include a focus on concept development, the use of multiple methods and materials to promote children's learning, and a variety of activities to encourage analysis, reasoning, and problem solving.[23] Both curricula specify that children should spend considerable time at activity centers, like those in Ms. Settles's classroom, playing in groups at activities designed to teach critical skills. The DEC team further enriched the curriculum by adding a "Building Communities" component aimed at teaching children the negotiation skills essential for constructive play and learning.

Recognizing that implementing these curricula well would pose a substantial challenge for most BPS preK teachers and require significant preparation for each lesson, DEC embarked on a multiyear strategy to increase the quality and consistency of instruction in preK classrooms. A first step was to provide teachers with manuals on how to prepare for and teach each of the many daily lessons in the curriculum. The manuals, which teachers could access online, described the goals of each lesson, provided a list of needed materials, offered guidelines about sequencing large- and small-group components, included a list of activities for small-group time, and offered suggestions for engaging children in thought processes that would increase their vocabulary and conceptual knowledge. For example, the scope and sequencing manual indicated that teachers should introduce *The Little Red Hen Makes a Pizza* in early November. It also specified the materials that should be present at the art table, the sand and water tables, and other centers, and it provided the activities that the teacher and her aide should offer at each center.

Each preK teacher received the educational supports she needed to implement the curriculum fully. This meant working with the facilities department to place a sink with running water in each preK classroom and to provide carpeting for the blocks corner to muffle the noise of falling structures. Sachs and his colleagues also provided all teachers with kits containing all of the materials they needed to carry out the full set of activities prescribed for each lesson. For example, the kit contained the playdough and plastic replicas of vegetables needed for the pizza-making activities. Without these materials, some teachers would skip the small-group play that the Early Childhood group recognized as critical to children's learning.

A third element of the quality improvement strategy was to provide the staffing necessary to implement the curriculum appropriately. This required building understanding and trust with principals, some of whom were inclined to assign their weakest teachers to preK classes. Over time, Sachs countered this tendency through a variety of actions. He organized and led professional development for school principals, explaining why the early childhood period is so important and what good teacher practice in early childhood classrooms looks like. He presented evidence that children who experienced a strong preK program fared better in the primary grades than those who had either no preK or a poor preK experience.

Sachs also recruited a former BPS principal, Ben Russell, which increased the credibility of DEC with principals and encouraged those with preK teaching vacancies to call the office for recommendations about promising candidates.

Also key was a full-time paraprofessional in each preK classroom to assist a licensed teacher. Without the paraprofessional, Sachs explained, teachers would be distracted by bathroom breaks and other interruptions and unable to teach the rich, time-intensive curriculum fully. Moreover, the paraprofessionals could improve the quality of children's learning experience by engaging children in vocabulary-rich conversations at one activity center while the teacher was doing the same thing with children at another center.

A fourth element of the improvement strategy was intense coaching and professional development aimed at providing all preK teachers and aides with the skills and knowledge to implement the demanding curricula. Part of the challenge was to convince teachers and aides that four-year-olds learn by doing, not by listening to teachers talk. Classroom management skills were also critical if children were to thrive in a cooperative learning setting. Yet another concern was to help teachers assess children's mastery of the skills and knowledge that provided the focus for the day's activities.

To achieve these objectives, DEC provided each preK teacher with professional development, including training over the summer in how to use the curricular materials. During the school year, the teachers spent several hours per month working with coaches to ensure that they were implementing the curriculum properly. The training was provided by a team of well-educated, experienced, ethnically diverse coaches, some of whom had worked for BPS and some for community-based preK programs. Having a mix of backgrounds on the coaching team was important in providing each teacher with the specific help she needed, as revealed by the Wellesley Centers's classroom evaluations.

Marina Boni is one of those coaches. It is quickly apparent that she gives careful thought to the structure of teaching and student activities. During our visit to Ms. Settles's classroom, the class seemed very engaged with the story of *The Little Red Hen Makes a Pizza*. Little did we know that it was part of an elaborate plan, which is clear from Boni's description of what she looks for when she visits classrooms:

> When I observe story time in a classroom, I should be able to tell whether it's the first, the second, or third, or a fourth read. During the first read the teacher is reading the book without interruptions, trying to give the children a full sense of the story and emphasizing specific vocabulary [words] that are key in order for the children to grasp the content of the story. For example, "delicatessen" . . . [is] a very unusual, complex word that the kids may not be . . . familiar with yet. The teachers might say something like, "She went to a delicatessen. A delicatessen is a special kind of store where they sell foods like special cheeses and meats and it's not like a supermarket. It's usually a small store."
>
> During the second read the teachers help the children recollect the story by engaging them in telling what they remember is happening or what might be happening next.
>
> During the third reading, the children are chiming in—you would imagine they are pretty familiar with the pattern of the book so they are able to read along with the teacher.
>
> The fourth read is an opportunity for reenacting the story. [*The Little Red Hen Makes a Pizza*] is a perfect example because there are distinct characters, the text is pretty repetitive, and the kids love to play the parts while the teacher is reading or retelling the story. Some teachers seize this opportunity and make costumes with the children and design the set. [It] can be a really engaging experience for the children.

When we asked Boni how the teachers learn to teach the very detailed curriculum, she explained that the key to success was to tailor coaching to individual needs, since teachers had different experience and teaching styles. For some teachers, it took time to become comfortable sitting at eye level with the children and reading stories in an expressive manner that engaged children's attention. Others needed to learn to give the children the freedom to choose activities, and to encourage them to try new things. Still others had difficulty managing transitions, especially cleaning up. As Marina explained,

> You have twenty-two kids, and seven or eight areas are open, blocks are everywhere, paints are everywhere . . . How am I going to get [the kids] to

clean up? Teachers really worry about the possibility that the children will not clean up, but the idea would be to teach the children strategies that help them remember what they are supposed to do. You might be giving the kids cues or warnings, which let them know that it's about time to clean up.

I want to help teachers to think more intentionally about how the areas/centers are set up so that the children are using the materials more purposefully rather than making gigantic messes because they don't know what to do with blocks or paint.

Another element of the quality improvement strategy was ongoing, independent assessment of instruction and of children's skills. Sachs contracted with the Wellesley Centers for Women for biennial evaluations of the preK system. He also provided the preK teachers with the results of the classroom evaluations. The underlying principle was that in order to improve their instruction, teachers needed to understand what they were and were not doing well. The data from the evaluations also showed what district-level changes were needed, such as providing time for the early childhood teachers to collaborate on developing instructional plans. Beginning in 2008, Sachs also began measuring children's vocabulary and language skills in a variety of ways. The DEC team needed regular updates on children's skills to know whether their efforts were achieving success.

A final, ongoing step in the effort to improve quality has been to seek accreditation from the National Association for the Education of Young Children (NAEYC). The NAEYC standards describe best practices for promoting children's intellectual growth and healthy development. The three-year accreditation process begins with a self-assessment aimed at identifying gaps between the school's current preK program and NAEYC benchmark standards. Action is then taken to correct deficiencies and improve the program until it meets the NAEYC standards. The accreditation process is expensive—$80,900 per school, or roughly $5,000 per classroom per year. However, Sachs believed it is worth the money because it provides a structured process for improvement, not only for preK classrooms, but also for kindergarten classrooms.

The value of the NAEYC accreditation process is borne out by evaluation data, which show that both the quality of the classroom learning environment and student outcomes improved in the schools that sought NAEYC accreditation. Sachs has been able to secure a grant from a local foundation to assist the growing number of BPS schools that request permission to go through the process. As of December 2011, BPS schools providing more than half of all early childhood classrooms have either received NAEYC accreditation for their preK programs or are currently working to achieve it.

THE EVALUATION EVIDENCE

Evidence shows that the BPS preK program has been successful. In 2006, 2008, and 2010, the Wellesley Centers for Women research team observed almost one hundred preK and kindergarten classrooms for three to four hours each, using established assessment tools to rate the quality of the environment, the curriculum, and instructional practices in the classes. In sharp contrast to 2006, almost two-thirds of BPS preK classrooms in 2010 met the "good" benchmark for environment, which means that they provided several well-resourced learning centers and opportunities for children to exercise choice and initiative. The research team also found that in more than one-half of BPS preK classrooms, "teachers supported children's oral language development, incorporated shared book reading and discussion of books daily, as well as provided informal opportunities for children to explore, read and hear books throughout the classroom and throughout the day. In these classrooms, teachers were regularly available to support and encourage all children's writing efforts, including dictation, writing group stories, and children's real and pretend writing."[24]

Of course, the critical question is whether four-year-olds enrolled in the BPS preK program are acquiring important skills and knowledge at a more rapid rate than they would have without the program. This question is particularly important in a period of tight school district budgets, given that the average annual cost of the Boston preK program is about $12,000 per student, with much of the cost stemming from staffing each preK classroom with both a teacher and an aide, both paid according to the BPS salary schedule. The results show that the program is indeed making a difference. Children who had participated in the BPS preK program scored higher on the state language arts test in grade three than nonparticipants.

Furthermore, the black-white achievement gap was one-third smaller among preK participants than among nonparticipants.[25]

Even more telling is an impact evaluation conducted by two Harvard researchers, Christina Weiland and Hiro Yoshikawa.[26] They found that the mathematics, literacy, and language skills of children who participated in the preK program were considerably more advanced than those of similarly-aged children who spent the year in other child-care settings.[27] Moreover, the evaluation also found improvements in executive functioning.[28] All in all, the size of the preK impacts was sufficient to close more than half of the gap at kindergarten entry between the academic skills of children from low-income families and those from relatively affluent ones.

ONGOING CHALLENGES

In recent years, the Boston Public Schools have made significant progress toward the goal of a universally available, consistently high-quality preK program. Yet many challenges remain. One is the prosaic but often difficult problem of space. PreK classrooms need to be near bathrooms. They need running water. In addition, there should be at least two preK classrooms in any given school so each preK teacher has a colleague. Finding space to meet these requirements in Boston's many old elementary school buildings has been difficult.

Another challenge has been finding an adequate supply of teachers who understand how young children learn and who can quickly develop the skills needed to implement the curriculum. Sachs and his colleagues have found that effective teachers use a number of different approaches to promote children's learning, including developing concepts, connecting them to the real world, and encouraging children to experiment, brainstorm, and make predictions.

Coaching and ongoing professional development have helped many teachers master these complex teaching tasks, but implementation quality still varies across classrooms. It has not been easy to find excellent coaches like Marina Boni. As Sachs said, "I just don't know how to scale strong, diverse, inspiring coaches." DEC staff are trying to solve this problem by using technology to provide teachers with easy-to-access videos illustrating how to teach particular lessons effectively.

A final challenge has been to meet the logistical needs of parents' work schedules. Moving from a half-day to a full 9:00 a.m. to 3:00 p.m. schedule made the preK program attractive to many parents, but others have jobs that require before- or afterschool care. Since most schools have been unable to extend the school day, many of these parents have not been able to enroll their children in the BPS preK program.

THE BIG PICTURE

As we documented in chapter 3, large gaps between the academic skills of children from low- and higher-income families are present at the beginning of kindergarten. These gaps persist through elementary school and high school, undermining poor children's ability to succeed in school. And success in school is essential for escaping poverty as an adult.

One reason that these skill gaps are present at school entry is that enrollment in preschool programs remains highly unequal. For more than forty years, enrollment rates in centers that provide some kind of developmental or educational focus have been 10 to 20 percentage points lower for children from families in the bottom half of the income distribution than for those whose families are in the top quarter. [29]

Spurred by discoveries from neuroscientists about the importance of early childhood education, as well as evidence from small-scale programs such as Perry Preschool and the Abecedarian Program, a growing number of states have sought to improve access to early learning among low-income children by introducing public prekindergarten programs. As of 2011, thirty-nine states funded preschool programs that collectively serve 28 percent of the nation's four-year-olds, up from 14 percent in 2002. [30] Quality has also improved over the last decade. In 2011, public preK programs in twenty states met at least eight of ten quality benchmarks. [31]

The Boston preK program shows that it is possible to develop and sustain a high-quality public preK program in a large urban school district, and that providing a rich, research-based curriculum along with coaching and professional development can help to close a substantial portion of the gap between poor and nonpoor children in school readiness.

It is important to acknowledge a few caveats, however. One question is whether districts that are unable to muster the same kinds of resources will be able to replicate the impacts from the well-designed and well-run Boston preK program. Boston's program provides more in-depth training for its teachers than many other preK programs, costs considerably more, and devotes considerably more resources to the quality implementation of its proven literacy and math curricula. So it is not surprising that its impacts are somewhat larger than those found in evaluations of preK programs in other states.[32]

Another key policy question is whether publicly funded preK programs—whether they be Boston's top-of-the-line model or the less expensive versions implemented in most states—are worthy social investments in the sense of generating more benefits than costs. At this time, preK programs simply have not been around long enough to be able to determine long-term benefits. That said, the impressive evidence from Boston demonstrates that well-designed and well-implemented preK programs have the potential to be a vital component of a strategy to improve the life chances of children from low-income families.

From a policy perspective, it is especially important to note that the programs with the strongest evidence of impacts—Boston and Tulsa—are open to children from all backgrounds, irrespective of family income. This may have increased the quality of these two programs and boosted the school readiness for economically disadvantaged children more than is the case with income-based programs—even though this strategy may also increase costs. Universal access also expands the constituency for preK programs, which may provide a base of political and financial support. Given the difficult funding situation most urban school districts currently face, one policy worth considering is to establish a sliding scale of fees for universal preK programs, with very low fees for low-income families and higher fees for families with more income.

Developing a high-quality preschool program in Boston has required considerable resources and time and a relentless focus on quality improvement. As in other promising interventions featured in this book, the program involves a carefully planned system of supports combined with accountability. Key supports include a high-quality curriculum, sufficiently high salaries to attract and retain well-educated teachers, extensive professional development and coaching, and the physical facilities and materials needed to engage children in the many learning activities that are part of the curriculum. Accountability for teachers was apparent in the periodic observation, evaluation, and coaching from principals and coaches, from the classroom component of the biennial evaluations conducted by the Wellesley Centers for Women, and from Jason Sach's goal of securing NAEYC accreditation for all of the classrooms.

Evaluation evidence from the Boston program supports the conclusion that providing low-income children with this kind of prekindergarten experience will allow them to enter kindergarten much better prepared to take advantage of what schools have to offer—potentially enabling schools to make a much bigger difference in setting these students up for success. The next challenge is to create elementary schools and high schools that can build on this foundation and, even more difficult, to meet the needs of children who have entered school at a disadvantage.

6

Elementary Schools
That Work

IT'S 9:00 ON A TUESDAY MORNING, and Erica Emmendorfer is teaching her first-grade class about "Bossy Rs." Emmendorfer is in her fifth year at the North Kenwood/Oakland (NKO) campus of the University of Chicago Charter School—where Shannon Keys, introduced in chapter 1, teaches as well. Emmendorfer's twenty-six students, all but two of whom are African American, are sitting on a rug of brightly colored squares. Ms. Erica, as the children call her, is reminding them that a "Bossy R" follows a vowel, forcing it to change its sound.

Pointing to words on a large poster, Emmendorfer reads the tongue twister of the week: "In the barn the girl on the horse had a bird in her purse." She asks the children to read the sentence aloud, concentrating on the sounds, and then to pick out the words that contain a "Bossy R." Several hands go up, and a child correctly points to the word "horse." After asking the child to pronounce the word, Emmendorfer reinforces the correct pronunciation and asks the children to repeat it. This mini-lesson is focused on developing the first graders' spelling, pronunciation, and reading fluency.[1] It is taking place during morning meeting, which marks the beginning of each day at NKO and precedes the two-hour literacy block devoted to developing children's reading and writing skills.

Up the stairs from Emmendorfer's classroom, Sarah Nowak, an energetic young teacher in her fourth year at NKO, is administering the Strategic

Teaching and Evaluation of Progress (STEP) reading assessment to one of the twenty-six African American children in her third-grade class. She asks the child to read a section of a book aloud so that she can assess his reading speed, accuracy, and fluency. He then finishes reading the book silently and writes down the answers to a set of questions, some of which require paragraph-length responses. Finally, Nowak asks the child additional questions to check for comprehension. She will repeat the process with increasingly challenging books until the child arrives at one that is too difficult. Using the assessment and a data management system, Nowak is able to evaluate the child's reading skills and determine his current level on a scale of thirteen literacy steps.

All preK through third grade teachers at NKO use STEP literacy assessments, conducted three times a year, to form guided reading groups. The two-hour literacy block, the daily mini-lessons, and guided reading groups are central elements of the balanced literacy curriculum in place at this charter school. STEP assessments also guide afterschool tutoring sessions where interns help children hone their skills.

While Nowak is administering the STEP assessment, other children are writing answers to questions about the types of books they have read recently, how much they read at home, and whether they find some kinds of books more interesting now than they did at the beginning of the year. A similar "reading interview" was conducted when school began in the fall. Nowak will compare the responses to assess the development of each child's reading tastes and skills.

After finishing the interview, some of the children are practicing skills using Study Island computer software. Others are reading the books they have chosen for the week. Still others are quietly searching for a "just right" book to read next, using the "five finger" choice method that Nowak taught them. As they read a page, they count the number of unknown words. If the count gets to five, the book is probably too difficult. If the count is zero or one, the book is too easy. A count of two or three means that the book is probably "just right." As a child starts to interrupt a classmate's reading, Nowak reminds him that talking is not allowed in the reading zone. She had introduced the reading zone concept at the beginning of the year, explaining that while in that area, each child should feel like the only person in the room, in the book with the characters.[2]

These elements—a coordinated focus on literacy across all grades, regular assessments of students' skills, and the use of the results to guide instructional improvement and identify students in need of remediation—are intentional components of the curriculum and philosophy of the University of Chicago Charter School network. The university's Urban Education Institute (UEI) leads this effort through its charter management organization (CMO) and its teacher and leader training programs.[3] The network has four campuses, two of which, including NKO, are K–5 elementary schools, while one is a middle school and the fourth is for grades six through twelve. As a charter school campus, NKO is exempt from some of the regulations that govern conventional public schools. However, it is required to administer the annual Illinois Standards Achievement Test (ISAT) to all students in grades K–8. In order to renew its charter every five years, the school needs to demonstrate that its students are performing adequately on the ISAT, which measures proficiency in reading and mathematics.

As with all charter schools, NKO is required to use a public lottery to select its students from the applications submitted by parents. Any child living in Chicago is eligible, but those living in the vicinity of the school are given preference. While there was little competition for enrollment when NKO first opened its doors, since relatively few families were aware of the school, this changed quickly. In 2011, six hundred children applied for the sixty slots in NKO's preK and kindergarten classes.

Although lotteries leave losers frustrated, they provide a transparent and powerful way to evaluate the school's effectiveness in developing children's reading and mathematical skills. Because lotteries are based on chance, the pool of successful candidates is statistically similar to that of unsuccessful applicants in terms of family background and levels of proficiency and motivation. This creates a natural experiment with a "treatment" and a "control" group. A research team led by eminent sociologist Stephen Raudenbush conducted an evaluation of the academic skills of the two groups and found significantly higher average reading and mathematics scores for children who had enrolled in a University of Chicago

Charter School after winning a lottery than for children who had lost the lottery and subsequently enrolled in another public school. In the case of reading achievement, the difference was thirty points on an SAT-type scoring scale, or roughly half of the overall gap between black and white children in the United States. The results for mathematics were even more striking—an average difference of forty points.[4]

For several reasons, we need to be cautious about drawing conclusions from the experience of NKO and the other University of Chicago Charter School campuses. This network of schools is very small and supported by one of the country's best universities, which is far from the norm. Moreover, the evaluation evidence is incomplete; for example, it is not yet clear whether children who attend one of the two elementary schools in the network fare better in the charter high school than students who enter the charter high school after graduating from a conventional Chicago public middle school.

While remembering these cautions, there are three reasons why the experiences of NKO and the other charter schools in its network provide insights about promising—and feasible—strategies to improve education in high-poverty schools. However one does the accounting, per-pupil expenditures in the charter school network are well within the range of typical per-student urban public school costs, so there is no obvious financial obstacle to adopting this model. Furthermore, the principal and teachers at NKO report that, while they work hard, their loads are sustainable. Unlike some successful schools whose strategies rely on the efforts of dedicated teachers who are able to put in long hours after school and on weekends, these schools do not require educators to sacrifice family commitments or other interests, and therefore promise to remain viable over the long run.

Third, and most important, the strategy developed by NKO and the other University of Chicago Charter School campuses to improve reading and mathematical skills is not unique; it is shared by virtually all schools that have shown long-term success in educating children from low-income families.[5] Like other such schools, the Chicago charter schools focus relentlessly on improving instruction and making it consistent across classrooms and grade levels. They select well-educated teachers who believe that all of their students can succeed. They institute and monitor a schoolwide set of norms for student behavior. They assess student skills frequently, and use the results both to guide instructional improvement and to identify students in need of skill remediation after school. Finally, they act quickly to address any problems with academics or behavior.[6]

THE EDUCATION CHALLENGE IN THE TWENTY-FIRST CENTURY

Why haven't more schools pursued the strategy that NKO and other successful high-poverty schools embrace? Part of the answer is that some of the findings underlying this strategy are quite new. For example, it has only been recognized in the last fifteen years or so that schools today need to teach all students to master skills that only a modest minority of students learned in the past. The NKO school improvement agenda is also informed by relatively recent research on child development and methods for preventing reading difficulties. In other words, we understand what has to happen in schools to prepare low-income children to thrive in twenty-first century America much better today than we did twenty years ago.

In addition, there are obstacles to implementing this strategy successfully. These include longstanding assumptions about the best way to organize schools and the work of teachers. As in Chris Zajac's Holyoke school (see chapter 4), teaching has been a private activity in most American schools. Teachers do the best they can to teach the skills students will need to succeed in the next grade. Most rely primarily on techniques their favorite teachers used.[7] As a result, children often learn the skills that were needed in the past, but not the problem-solving, literacy, and communication skills that are essential in today's labor market.[8]

Teachers often recognize that some students are not learning critical skills and want to help them. But they are already using everything they know and working as hard as they can. In-service training may introduce them to new teaching methods, but it rarely enables them to teach effectively in new, unfamiliar ways. Thus many teachers conclude that the best way they can serve their students is to continue to teach as they did in the past, even if it leaves some children without the skills they need for a successful future.

Since teaching is usually considered a private activity, with each teacher working independently, instruction and classroom management strategies vary widely even within the same school. A fifth-grade teacher may use a very different method to explain how to add dissimilar fractions from the one used by the teacher who taught the same children the previous year. Teachers' classroom management strategies and behavioral expectations also vary, as do their responses to misbehavior. The lack of consistency from classroom to classroom and from year to year confuses students and interferes with their learning.

Of course there are exceptional schools in which talented teachers work together to make instruction coherent and consistent, establish and maintain a uniform code of student conduct, and identify and address the lagging skills of individual children. Such schools tend to have an indefatigable, charismatic leader at the helm who is able to recruit teachers who are equally committed. However, the success of these schools often fades quickly when the leader moves on or when teachers, for whatever reason, are no longer able to devote almost every waking hour to the school.

District administrative structures are another weak link. Conventional public schools are usually part of a school district with a central office that is responsible for providing guidance, oversight, and resources. Where most central offices fall short is in their support of instructional improvement—the primary mission of schools. Unlike the University of Chicago's Urban Education Institute, most large districts fail to focus on implementing a consistent, research-based instructional program. There are several reasons why this is so. One is a governance structure under which locally elected school committees hire and fire school superintendents and approve budgets and programmatic initiatives. Some school committee members have goals—including gaining political power and obtaining jobs for relatives and friends—other than providing all children with the skills they will need to thrive in twenty-first century America.[9]

Another problem is the typically brief—less than four years—tenure of superintendents in urban districts serving high concentration of low-income families.[10] Most new superintendents want to launch new signature initiatives to make their mark on district policy. But since those superintendents are likely to move on before long, teachers and school leaders are often reluctant to embrace even promising initiatives because a new administrator will be right around the corner with yet another new agenda.

A further contributing factor is that most urban district central offices are large bureaucracies with many "silos." Each department has its own standard operating procedures and does not typically coordinate its work with other departments. The average district has hundreds of programs with different objectives and funding sources. Central offices administer the funding of these programs but rarely ask whether they contribute to a coherent instructional program.[11]

Anachronistic union contracts, too, may make it more difficult to improve teaching and learning. In almost all U.S. public school districts, teacher compensation is based on a schedule that exclusively rewards years of teaching experience and educational credentials. When first introduced more than fifty years ago, these uniform salary scales were a step forward from previous compensation practices that were rife with favoritism and race and gender biases. However, they do not support instructional improvement today, especially in high-poverty schools where the teaching challenge is especially great.

Union contract provisions that base access to transfers on seniority made sense in the past, but not today. Typically these provisions were introduced during the 1950s and 1960s when school districts were scrambling to find enough teachers to deal with burgeoning student enrollments. At that time, they were an inexpensive benefit aimed at retaining teachers. Now they make it more difficult to create an environment in which teachers work together over an extended period of time in the interest of more effective and consistent instruction. As described in chapter 4, the uniform salary scale and seniority-based transfers thus contribute to an all-too-common situation: schools serving the largest concentrations of low-income children tend to have the least experienced and most transient teaching staffs.

The challenge, therefore, is to create *systems* of schools that continue to improve and sustain school performance, help teachers learn together to serve students more effectively, and do so within a schedule that highly motivated, dedicated professionals can sustain. How have the University of Chicago Charter School campuses made progress toward this objective? For Tim Knowles, the director of the University of Chicago Urban

Education Institute, it begins with strong leaders and ample support. Knowles spent more than a year convincing Tanika Island-Smith, a talented elementary school literacy and social studies teacher with a reputation for supporting her colleagues, to leave her classroom and become director of NKO. She finally agreed when Knowles assured her that he would prepare her for this leadership role. The preparation involved shadowing an effective school principal for nearly a year and meeting weekly with Knowles and his UEI colleagues. Each meeting focused on particular aspects of the job of directing a learning organization, such as building a leadership team, using videotaping and classroom observations to make each teacher's instruction a shared resource, tailoring professional development to the needs of individual teachers, and building a school schedule that included grade-level planning time.

Recruiting Island-Smith to lead NKO and preparing her to do so effectively is just one example of the many ways in which the Urban Education Institute has supported NKO and the three other school campuses in its network. It also provides a comprehensive assessment system (STEP) to measure students' progress in reading, and coaches teachers extensively on the use of the balanced literacy approach and STEP reading assessment. UEI provides the four charter school campuses with afterschool tutors from its teacher education program and helps the schools recruit as teachers talented graduates, such as Erica Emmendorfer, who have extensive training in balanced literacy. The charter management organization also handles a host of time-consuming logistical issues, such as finding school buildings and negotiating with vendors for school lunches and health insurance. Finally, the CMO raises private funds to pay for important school activities such as the afterschool program. In other words, UEI provides the supports that NKO needs to continue to improve, and to do so in a manner that is sustainable for the school's teaching staff.

CHARTER SCHOOLS TO THE RESCUE?

Scholars find that it is much more difficult to change the culture and improve the performance of an existing organization (referred to as a brownfield) than it is to create a successful organization from scratch (a green-field). This is a factor behind the push in many states to increase the number of charter schools, like NKO. In chapter 9, we will address the promise—and dangers—of this widespread policy initiative. At this point, however, we focus on the evidence about the effectiveness of charter schools.

Some charter schools have produced dramatic improvements in their students' skills, but this is true of only a small percentage of charter schools.[12] The best available evidence suggests that most charter schools are no more effective than conventional public schools at improving the skills of low-income children.[13] As Steven Wilson, a former CEO of a group of charter schools and a charter school advocate, noted, "Advocates had expected that the structural advantages of charters—the new bargain extended to founders of authority and autonomy in exchange for accountability for results; the shared purpose that would result from faculty and students who had chosen the school, rather than been assigned to it; and the freedom from tenure and union contracts—would prove decisive. These privileges alone did not unleash a new generation of dramatically superior schools, as many charter programs had hoped."[14]

Charter schools face daunting tasks, including hiring promising teachers, developing a curriculum, and designing and implementing a code for student behavior. Then there are the logistical challenges: finding space, satisfying building codes, dealing with vendors for everything from health insurance to school lunches. Thus it may not be surprising that most charter schools are no more effective at educating disadvantaged children than conventional public schools have been.

Proponents of charters argue that the chartering authorities will close ineffective charter schools, and that entrepreneurs will successfully replicate those that prove effective. However, it is difficult to close ineffective charter schools because every school—even those that are not performing well—has vocal advocates.[15] As for replication, Wilson points out the limits to the replicability of the prominent "no excuses" charter school model, which relies on teachers with a strong undergraduate background devoting themselves virtually round the clock to improving their students' skills. How many teachers are willing to make that kind of sacrifice? In

Wilson's view, "going to scale" with effective charter schools will require the supports—expertise, guidance, resources—that the University of Chicago Charter School management provides to NKO.

The important lesson here is that individual schools, whether they are charter schools or conventional public schools, are not in a position to design and implement effective strategies for educating disadvantaged children. The work is simply too difficult. To become more effective, high-poverty schools need strong systems of supports tailored to their needs.

A growing recognition of the need for support has led to growth in the number and scale of organizations designed to play this guidance and support role for charter schools. Achievement First, Uncommon Schools, and Green Dot Public Schools are examples of charter management organizations that provide affiliated schools with school supports, including professional development for teachers, student assessment systems, and guidance in designing and implementing codes of student behavior.[16] It remains to be seen whether CMOs will be effective in providing the critical school supports that the growing number of charter schools will need to serve low-income children well.

HOW CAN WE BUILD SUPPORTING SYSTEMS?

We have pointed out that few, if any, urban school districts provide the necessary supports effectively and consistently.[17] In some cases, central offices lack the requisite funding. However, the problem more often lies in the organization and culture of central school district offices themselves, especially in cities with large low-income student populations. Over the long term, few provide the supports that the University of Chicago CMO offers NKO and the other three school campuses in its network.

Lessons from the University of Chicago Charter School Network

It is hardly fair to compare a CMO with responsibility for four schools with an urban school district central office responsible for several hundred. Yet it is worth asking whether an urban school district's central office could provide the same kinds of services as the University of Chicago CMO does. As for the recruitment and preparation of school leaders, there is no denying that the year-long preparation of Tanika Island-Smith to direct NKO was expensive. But it was no more so than the fifteen-month leadership preparation that the New York City public schools provided to Flavia Puello Perdomo, who will be introduced in the next chapter, and hundreds of other aspiring school leaders through the New York City Leadership Academy. New York City is only one of several urban school districts that are learning to recruit and prepare school leaders more effectively than in the past.

Another key element in NKO's system of school supports is a literacy coach who works full-time with teachers to help them implement the balanced literacy curriculum and the STEP formative assessment system. This too costs money, but probably adds up to no more than the total cost of the diverse professional development activities that school district central offices pay for. The difference is that for fourteen years, the University of Chicago CMO has maintained a consistent focus on improving the delivery of the balanced literacy curriculum. In that period, a typical urban school district would have had at least four superintendents, each of them likely to scrap prior initiatives and implement new ones.

Also costly is the STEP reading assessment, which provides valuable information to grade-level teams as they review the effectiveness of their instruction each week and target students for extra help. But many school districts spend money on frequent assessments of students' reading skills, yet those results rarely play a central role in planning instruction and targeting remediation, as they do at NKO.

The University of Chicago CMO also awards stipends to teachers who assume additional responsibilities. Third-grade teacher Sarah Nowak, for example, agreed to serve as science coordinator, a position that involves helping other NKO teachers improve their science instruction, and especially helping them to integrate literacy components into science instruction. As part of the effort to maintain a consistently positive school environment, first-grade teacher Erica Emmendorfer, a certified yoga teacher, agreed to teach other NKO teachers how to use yoga to calm restless children—something the children love, as it turns out. Both received extra pay for their efforts.

The benefits of these payments to NKO teachers for assuming leadership roles are far greater than those derived from conventional payments to teachers for master's degrees, which rarely affect the quality of teaching.[18]

The point here is not to suggest paying teachers less by removing pay premiums for educational credentials. In fact, as schools compete for talent, many high-poverty schools will need to pay higher salaries to attract and retained skilled teachers. The point is that pay premiums should be directed to activities that clearly benefit students.

Lessons from Comprehensive School Reform Design Organizations

Some of the most compelling evidence suggesting that it is possible to boost support for large numbers of high-poverty schools comes from organizations that have developed comprehensive school reform designs. In the late 1980s and early 1990s, several groups of school reformers and researchers developed comprehensive designs to improve high-poverty schools. Their approach was to intervene directly in schools by forming leadership teams, introducing new curricula, changing instructional methods, and using test results to place children in reading groups and identify those in need of targeted tutoring.[19]

The best known and most widely adopted comprehensive school reform design is Success for All (SFA). Developed by scholars at Johns Hopkins University, SFA was first introduced in a single Baltimore elementary school in 1987. By 2012, more than 1,100 schools, the vast majority of which serve high concentrations of low-income children, had begun to use Success for All. The SFA approach to reading instruction includes a schoolwide, daily ninety-minute reading block, clear instructions for teachers, grouping of students by skill level for reading instruction, frequent assessment of children's reading skills, and use of the results to identify children who need extra tutoring. The comprehensive, detailed structure of SFA is especially valuable when teachers have little experience and weak preparation.

America's Choice is another comprehensive school reform design that hundreds of high-poverty elementary schools have adopted. While it differs from SFA in significant respects, it also shares many elements, including a detailed reading curriculum, professional development focused on the implementation of the curriculum, and frequent assessments of children's skills.[20] The organizations that sponsor these comprehensive school reform designs provide some of the supports that are so critical to school improvement.

A number of studies have examined the effects of Success for All and America's Choice,[21] and we draw three lessons from their findings. The first is that large-scale improvement is indeed possible, since these two programs create comprehensive, concrete improvement strategies that are of value to teachers and school leaders in large numbers of high-poverty public schools.

The second is that the tools, guidance, and training that SFA and America's Choice provide for the teaching staffs of high-poverty schools have improved children's reading skills. The most rigorous evaluation of SFA found that after three years, elementary school students in SFA schools scored significantly higher on reading comprehension tests than did students in demographically similar schools that had not adopted SFA. Expressed on a SAT-type scale, the difference amounted to about twenty points.

Finally, these and other comprehensive school reform designs to improve children's education are much less effective when implemented in schools with a high level of teacher turnover and relatively unskilled teaching staffs working under very stressful conditions. This is an all-too-common situation in high-poverty schools. It is particularly difficult to achieve reforms when a comprehensive school design team is working at cross-purposes with a school district central office and a state department of education. Supervisory organizations often demand compliance with a variety of regulations that are not well aligned with the whole-school improvement effort.[22]

THE BIG PICTURE

Currently, only a very small proportion of the nation's low-income children attend elementary schools like NKO in which a stable group of well-educated teachers work together to improve the consistency and quality of instruction and pay close attention to the progress and development of every student. Instead, most attend schools in which teachers work in relative isolation under extremely difficult conditions. Because working conditions are difficult in a great many high-poverty schools, teacher turnover rates are high. Consequently, investments in improving teachers' skills fail to bear fruit.[23] As a result, a great many low-income children are deprived of the education they need to thrive in twenty-first-century America.

Improving the education of low-income students requires systems of strong supports for high-poverty schools, including access to well-educated teachers who want to work with low-income children, guidance about how to create and sustain a culture of continuous improvement and shared responsibility, and access to the necessary expertise and resources for educating these children. Well-designed accountability is an essential complement to a system of strong supports. For NKO, accountability takes two forms. One is responsibility for increasing the percentage of its students who score at the proficient or advanced level on the state's annual mandatory English and mathematics examinations. A second and more immediate form of accountability is the responsibility to keep one's classroom door open to coaches, peers, and school leaders, and to work with them to make instruction better and more consistent. In chapter 9 we will discuss school supports and accountability in greater detail.

We don't yet know what the impact of schools like NKO will be on the life chances of low-income children. Short-term impacts on student achievement look promising, but long-term studies like those conducted for early childhood education program have not yet been undertaken. What we do know is that NKO focuses on more than just basic skills, and that it strives to create the conditions for continuous improvement in both teaching and learning. As we await longer-run evidence, we can learn a great deal by observing whether high-poverty schools are able to attract and retain well-educated teachers like Shannon Keys, Erica Emmendorfer, and Sarah Nowak and skilled leaders like Tanika Island-Smith. Only through the coordinated and sustained efforts of educators like these can schools improve the life chances of low-income children.

7

High Schools That Improve Life Chances

JOSE RUBIO AND HIS MOTHER, MARIANA, live in the South Bronx—one of the poorest and most crime-ridden neighborhoods in New York City.[1] Mariana had wanted to send Jose to a Catholic high school because of its reputation for a close-knit community and academic rigor. However, she had resigned herself to sending Jose to a public high school because she could not afford the private school tuition. A decade earlier, Jose would have been assigned to South Bronx High School, a large comprehensive school where only one in three students graduated. By 2008, however, when Jose was entering high school, South Bronx High had closed. The New York City school system now required eighth graders to select their top choices from several hundred schools listed in the Directory of the New York City Public High Schools, ranking them in order of preference.

Born into a low-income Latino family, Jose faced stiff odds against finishing high school and attending college. As we saw in chapter 3, at school entry U.S. children whose families are in the bottom 20 percent of the income distribution score, on average, more than a standard deviation lower on math and reading tests than children in the top 20 percent. They gain little ground by the time they enter high school, and one out of every three fails to graduate.[2] Among Latino males, the statistics are even more troubling, with only three in five graduating from high school.[3]

Mariana Rubio was attracted to nearby Mott Haven Village Preparatory High School because the word "village" suggested an emphasis on community. She and Jose attended an open house, where they learned that MHV Prep, one of three small public high schools located in the building that had once housed South Bronx High School, did indeed emphasize community as well as academic rigor and preparation for college. Impressed by what they heard from MHV Prep's teachers, Mariana and Jose listed the school as his top choice, and the computer-based system that matched students' rankings with school openings offered him a place there. It proved to be a good choice. MHV Prep provided a strong, caring community, which was exactly what Mariana was seeking for her son. As Jose commented in the fall of his senior year, "Whether you're like outgoing or shy, every teacher knows your name, every teacher knows what you're capable of, every teacher knows your potential and they make you feel really at home. So, it's like my second home away from home."

Eleven miles away, in downtown Brooklyn, high school senior Ashanti Baker expressed similar enthusiasm for her small public school of choice, the Urban Assembly School for Law and Justice (SLJ). Ashanti, a petite young African American, travels an hour by bus and train each morning to reach SLJ from her home in another part of Brooklyn. She values the school's attention to detail in preparing students for college, noting that "teachers hunt you down to go to the college office." Ashanti also likes the school's dress code because it saves her time in the morning. SLJ is making a difference in the lives of its 450 students, virtually all of whom are black or Latino, most from low-income families. In 2012, 86 percent of SLJ's students graduated and enrolled in college.[4]

The successes of Mott Haven Village Prep and the Urban Assembly School for Law and Justice are not unique. Indeed, the nation's newspapers regularly feature articles about schools in low-income neighborhoods that "beat the odds," at least for a few years. What is unique, however, is that MHV Prep and SLJ were established as part of a comprehensive effort to create and support more than two hundred small high schools in low-income New York City neighborhoods. The scale of this effort is remarkable, as is the fact that it happened in a public school district legendary for its stifling bureaucracy. Most impressive, a high-quality evaluation of the entire effort (discussed later in this chapter) showed that these small schools of choice have markedly improved high school graduation rates for New York City youth from low-income families.

In this chapter, we focus on the systemic initiative that has made it possible for tens of thousands of low-income New York City youth to obtain a higher-quality secondary education. Our purpose is not to advocate for this particular approach; other approaches, such as career academies and early-college high schools, also show promise for educating low-income students.[5] Instead, we show some of the hows and whys of creating and sustaining networks of high schools that do an effective job of serving economically disadvantaged youth, even those who enter ninth grade with extremely weak academic skills. The key message is that it is indeed possible to design high schools that improve the skills and graduation rates of low-income youth on a scale that goes beyond a handful of innovative examples, and in even the largest urban school districts. We describe the challenges that educators and education systems must meet to create and sustain a network of effective schools, and we identify the elements of a strategy that has made a real difference.

DRAWING ON THE PAST

The architects of new high school options for thousands of New York City teenagers did not start from scratch. Instead, their design drew hard-learned lessons from earlier attempts to improve high school education in the city. New York has a history of creating small public high schools that serve disadvantaged students. One of the best known is Central Park East, which pioneering educator Deborah Meier founded in 1985 to serve youth in East Harlem. The number of small high schools in New York City grew during the 1990s, thanks in part to the efforts of Meier and her colleagues, and in part to a large grant from the Annenberg Foundation to replace dysfunctional large schools with smaller ones. But while many of these small schools continue to operate and, in some cases, thrive, their number remained modest relative to the scope of the challenges facing the city. Hopes that the creation of several dozen effective small high schools would catalyze district-wide reforms were unfulfilled, largely because of a lack of a cogent framework for structuring these schools. Consequently, the new small schools funded by the Annenberg Challenge had little in common with one another and failed to gain traction as a structured alternative to New York's large comprehensive high schools.

For the small schools operating during the 1990s, the attitude of the central school administration was even more problematic. The administration viewed them as exceptions in a system of centralized control, tolerating them only because they pacified innovative educators who would otherwise have been more vocal critics of the system.[6] Not only did the central office lack a strategy to support small schools, its routine operations made it difficult for them to be effective. Departing leaders of small schools were sometimes replaced with new principals who did not share the school's vision. Schools that depended on a small, close-knit faculty to develop strong personal ties with students were frustrated by provisions in the New York City teachers' contract allowing teachers who had lost their positions because of enrollment cuts to "bump" less senior teachers from their positions in other schools.

Although the Annenberg effort met with mixed success, it laid essential groundwork for the New Century High Schools initiative that followed. One critical legacy was a group of educators who had worked in small schools and knew what it takes to build and sustain them. Another was a group of not-for-profit organizations with experience in creating networks of small schools. One of them, New Visions for Public Schools, played a central role in designing and leading the New Century High Schools initiative.

NEW CENTURY HIGH SCHOOLS

After decades of work developing school-community collaborations, Michele Cahill signed on in 1999 as a senior program officer at the Carnegie Corporation of New York, a large philanthropic organization. Cahill saw great potential for small high schools to do a better job of educating disadvantaged youth, especially if they had strong community partners that would provide students with learning opportunities and resources. Mindful of the mixed success of small schools in urban districts, Cahill set out to design a small-high-schools initiative that would build on lessons learned from previous efforts. She enlisted the support of Robert Hughes, a public-interest lawyer who became president of New Visions for Public Schools in September 2000. New Visions, a not-for-profit organization founded in 1989, had worked throughout the 1990s to engage low-income communities in improving education in the city. It had also facilitated the creation of many small schools under the Annenberg Challenge.

Together Cahill, Hughes, and their collaborators developed a plan for launching successful small high schools in the city. The initiative, which became known as New Century High Schools, was funded by Carnegie, the Gates Foundation, and the Open Society Institute, and was administered by New Visions. One of Bob Hughes's first acts was to form a "Core Team" that included representatives of the three foundations, the Board of Education, and the unions representing teachers and school administrators (the United Federation of Teachers and the Council of Supervisors and Administrators, respectively). The Core Team met monthly to work out operational plans for creating New Century Schools, taking into account the rights of teachers and administrators who worked in the large comprehensive high schools that would be closed.

Early in 2001, New Visions invited not-for-profit groups to submit proposals for $50,000 planning grants to create new small schools with characteristics it viewed as fundamental for success: a rich and rigorous curriculum, personalization, effective teaching and learning, and clear pathways to post-secondary education, careers, and community participation.[7] The request for proposals (RFP) included three provisions designed to ensure that New Century High Schools would not be isolated from their surrounding communities. First, funding for the planning and implementation of a new school would go to the lead community partner rather than to the school directly. This signaled that the designers envisioned a much closer relationship between schools and community partners than is common in the United States. Second, responses to the RFP had to be submitted by the district superintendent rather than by the group proposing the new school. And third, New Visions offered technical supports to potential applicants, including help in finding promising community partners, arranging site visits to successful small schools, and holding workshops on writing proposals.

To launch the initiative, Hughes approached Norman Wechsler, the superintendent for Bronx high schools, to see if he would be willing to close some large dysfunctional high schools and replace them with smaller New Century high schools. Wechsler agreed and recruited long-time New York City educator Eric Nadelstern to spearhead the process as deputy superintendent for new and small Bronx high schools.

Nadelstern was a brilliant choice. A native New Yorker with more than twenty-five years of experience as a teacher and principal in the city, he understood the system. In 1985 Nadelstern had founded an extremely effective small high school for recent immigrants. He also lived in the Bronx and knew that despite the poor performance of its high schools, the borough contained many talented educators and community-based organizations committed to school improvement. The challenge was to bring together the latent talent, catalyze the development of partnerships, and guide the partners through the school development process.

After several months of hard work, thirty-four teams submitted proposals for new small schools. In January 2002, the Core Team approved fifteen of the proposals. With support from Nadelstern's office and New Visions, the winning teams used their grants to accomplish the many tasks involved in opening a new school, including selecting teachers, recruiting students, and creating curricula. In September 2002, twelve New Century High Schools in the Bronx opened their doors to a first class of ninth graders. The following year another eighteen small schools opened in the Bronx and Brooklyn.[8]

Mott Haven Village Prep

Josué Rodriguez, the associate executive director of East Side House Settlement, was the leader of one of the teams that submitted a successful proposal. East Side House, a nonprofit community-based organization, had a long history of providing services to residents of the South Bronx. Among them was an afterschool program at Mott Haven Village School (PS 220), a prekindergarten to grade 8 neighborhood public school that New Visions had created during the 1990s. Rodriguez and Stefan Zucker, the principal of PS 220, had long dreamed of creating a small high school that would serve PS 220's graduates. John Sanchez, the executive director of East Side House, recognized the opportunity the New Century High Schools competition had created and authorized Rodriguez to explore that possibility.

To develop the proposal, Rodriguez recruited a planning team that included parents, students, East Side House staff members, Zucker, and Ana Maldonado, a fifth-grade teacher with more than twenty years of experience who at that time ran one of Eastside House's afterschool programs. Three months later, the planning team led by Rodriguez submitted a proposal for a new small high school with a "strong curriculum that integrates humanities and natural science with community service and environmental awareness." [9]

Once the proposal was approved, the real work began. Rodriguez and Sanchez asked Ana Maldonado to serve as the school's principal for at least five years. She was an unusual choice, as she and Eric Nadelstern pointed out, since her teaching experience was confined to elementary and middle schools, and she had never been a public school administrator. Rodriguez and Sanchez were undeterred, however, as they valued the leadership skills that Maldonado had demonstrated in her work with East Side House. After assurances that East Side House was committed to the new high school for the long haul, Maldonado agreed to become its founding principal.

The Mott Haven Village team worked feverishly for the next six months. Maldonado and Rodriguez visited middle schools in the Bronx to recruit students, assuring them that Mott Haven Village Prep would prepare them to enroll and succeed in college, irrespective of their current grades. The team made it clear that MHV Prep would be a community committed to each student's success. There would be a dress code, and students would be expected to work hard and treat all members of the community with respect. In return, the school and its partners would provide them with abundant opportunities to acquire the knowledge and skills they would need to succeed in college. The trust that East Side House had earned among residents of the South Bronx lent credibility to the promises made in the recruitment pitch, and an initial class of eighty-five ninth graders enrolled in the school.

The promised combination of community, caring, rigor, and opportunities is important. The transition from childhood to adolescence brings with it a host of physical, emotional, and neurological changes that are often at odds with the structure of middle and high schools.[10] Adolescents are in special need of close relationships with adults outside of their homes. However, in large comprehensive middle and high schools, teachers see as many as 175 students each day. This structure forces teachers to focus on logistical concerns and subject content, at the expense of interpersonal connections with students.

Many adolescents have fragile and malleable self-perceptions, and their concern about status relative to peers is ill served by the ability-level tracking common in large comprehensive high schools. An adolescent's need for more complex academic tasks is often left unsatisfied by instructional methods that focus on preparation for standardized tests. And just when students are becoming increasingly eager for self-determination, participation in rule making, and emotional support, schools tend to resort to rigid disciplinary policies. Moreover, many urban teens living in low-income neighborhoods fear for their safety. One common response is to join a gang, which may offer some protection against violence, but often at the expense of attention to schoolwork. MHV Prep sought to provide an educational alternative more closely aligned with the needs of urban, low-income adolescents for respect, opportunities to do meaningful work—both in school and with community partners—and close personal relationships with adults who are committed to helping them succeed.

Fulfilling these goals required skilled, dedicated teachers. Of course, the team wanted to find teachers who knew their subject matter and how to teach it. But the teachers also needed to share the belief that South Bronx youth could succeed in college, and they needed to be determined to make that happen. After rigorous screening of applicants that included teaching a demonstration class at PS 220, the middle school led by Stefan Zucker, the team hired five teachers.

Over July and August the new teachers and the planning team developed the ninth-grade curriculum. Since Mott Haven's students would need to pass the state's Regents examinations in core subject areas, those examinations played a large role in structuring the curriculum. The planning team also created a schedule that included twice a week advisories—sessions in which a small group of students met with a faculty member to work on study habits, strategies for conflict resolution, and other issues of concern. The schedule also included opportunities for students to use the up-to-date computer laboratory at East Side House and participate in the organization's College Preparatory and Leadership Program.

The Urban Assembly School for Law and Justice

While MHV Prep has its roots in the East Side House initiative, the School for Law and Justice had a somewhat different beginning. In 1990 Richard Kahan, a New Yorker with an admirable track record of tackling urban problems by fostering partnerships between the public and private sectors, founded the Urban Assembly. Its mission was to promote economic development. In 1997 Kahan responded to the Annenberg Challenge by creating one small high school. At that time Kahan saw the school as a "one off" deviation from the Urban Assembly's core mission. However, like Cahill, he came to recognize that good public schools are an essential component of economic development, and in 2001 he accepted an invitation from Bob Hughes to submit proposals for New Century High Schools. The Urban Assembly School for Law and Justice, which opened in 2004 with the prestigious law firm of Cravath, Swaine & Moore LLP as its lead partner, is one of twenty high schools in the Urban Assembly's network of small schools of choice in New York City.

In many ways SLJ's initial challenges were similar to those facing MHV Prep and the other New York City small schools of choice: to set up facilities, design curriculum, recruit staff and students, and comply with a host of bureaucratic regulations. Just as East Side House played a central role in helping MVP Prep get on its feet, the Urban Assembly did so for SLJ. One of many questions that the Urban Assembly helped SLJ to resolve was the extent to which its theme, law and justice, should dominate the curriculum. Too much emphasis on a theme can limit curriculum, while too little squanders students' initial enthusiasm, a major strength of themed schools. As it does with all of its schools, the Urban Assembly placed a full-time staff member on its own payroll at SLJ for the first two years, with responsibilities for engaging partners around the theme and finding meaningful intersections with curriculum, in ways that enriched and supplemented classroom learning without eclipsing or impeding it.

For senior Ashanti Baker, a typical Monday at SLJ starts with checking in with her advisor at 8:55 and catching up on news about events and activities. Then she goes to her Accelerated Geometry class, followed by Physics and Advanced Placement English. At noon is "advisory," a thirty-six-minute, three-times-per-week session with seventeen other seniors and an advisor, an SLJ teacher. This year Ashanti's advisory sessions have focused on skills needed for the college application process and life after SLJ. Students also meet one-on-one with their advisor when progress reports and report cards come out and any time a student is experiencing difficulty at home or in school. Advisories, which are also a part of a student's experience at Mott Haven Village Prep, are one way of ensuring that every student has at least one personal relationship with a caring adult.

After advisory, Ashanti has lunch, followed by Advanced Placement Microeconomics. Then comes Magazine Club, an activity that Ashanti started and leads. The group publishes a magazine for SLJ students with articles written by club members. Topics include current events, fashion trends, hair advice, and special topics such as what to wear to the prom.

Building Reading Skills

The faculties of the small high schools of choice in New York City embrace the goal of preparing all students to succeed in postsecondary education and training programs and to thrive in a rapidly changing society. However, they face much greater challenges in realizing this goal than do the faculties of schools serving primarily middle-class students. One of the most difficult challenge stems from the below-grade-level reading skills of a great many students entering the small high schools of choice.

About half of the students entering ninth grade at SLJ lack the reading skills to comprehend high school texts, and some read only at the third-

or fourth-grade level. Preparing these students to succeed in high school without reducing the quality of education provided to better prepared students is a central theme of the SLJ faculty's work. It begins with an intense focus on building literacy skills. All ninth graders take a double period class in English Language Arts. The sections of the class are not grouped by ability and all students participate in discussions of the same texts, which include Sophocles' *Antigone* and Steinbeck's *Of Mice and Men*. What does differ among students is their reading assignments. For example, while the better-prepared students read ten pages of *Antigone* for homework, students with very weak reading skills might be assigned to read a two-page summary of the same material prepared by the teachers. All of the students practice the same skills, which include asking questions about the text to bring to class, looking for answers in the text, and circling unfamiliar words. Students turn in their annotations and receive feedback from teachers on the quality of their thinking. Thirty minutes of the daily-double literacy block is devoted to Independent Reading, during which students read and take notes on a book they chose that fits their reading level, and teachers work with individual students on particular literacy skills and increasing their reading level. To be sure that instruction is consistent across sections and that no student is neglected, the two ninth-grade SLJ teachers plan every lesson together, teach the same lesson on the same day, administer the same diagnostic assessments, and look at student work together during their common planning time.

At SLJ, developing students' literacy skills is the work of all teachers, not just English teachers. For example, the ninth-grade science class is called Forensics, and focuses on teaching students the skills to read nonfiction science texts. Teaching students to read nonfiction social studies texts is a major focus of the ninth-grade government class. The teaching team at each grade level meets for ninety minutes every Wednesday, a day when students are dismissed early to provide time for this collaborative work. During the grade-level meetings, the teachers align strategies for teaching particular literacy skills, such as annotating text, across the content areas. Together they look at work done by individual students and develop intervention plans for lagging students that all teachers adopt. The goal of these grade-level meetings is to make instruction in specific literacy strategies coherent and consistent across the subject areas while also developing individualized plans for building the skills of lagging students.

SLJ also works on aligning the curriculum vertically so that instruction in each subject area builds on skills students learned in previous years. For example, to make writing instruction more consistent, the school's English teachers developed a strategy for teaching students to write paragraphs. The ninth-grade English teachers teach this TIDE strategy—Topic Sentence, Introduce Evidence, Discuss Evidence—to all students and all SLJ English teachers reinforce it in the higher grades.

Another dimension of the SLJ strategy for teaching students the literacy skills they need to pass the eleventh-grade Regents English examination, a requirement for graduation, is professional development for teachers. This is critical because, in SLJ principal Shannon Curran's words, "Nobody teaches you in an ed school when you are prepping to teach ninth or tenth grade how you teach a ninth or tenth grader that is reading at a second-grade level."[11] At SLJ, professional development is a collaborative activity focused particularly on teaching literacy strategies effectively. Principal Curran and Assistant Principal Suzette Dyer have found that the greatest buy-in comes when SLJ teachers learn from the most effective of their own colleagues. SLJ's master teachers, who are typically department heads, learn about new ideas and resources at workshops and conferences. They then use what they learn to hone their own instructional practices. In turn, SLJ teachers watch and discuss videos of the instructional practices of the master teachers at departmental and grade-level team meetings. They then work together developing and implementing plans to incorporate these instructional practices in their own teaching.

In summary, SLJ's strategy for serving students who enter high school with very weak reading and writing skills includes institutional structures that provide the time and focus for collaborative work, timely interventions to develop the skills of lagging students, and professional development to continually improve instruction and make it more coherent and consistent. Even with strong supports, the work is difficult. In Principal Curran's words, "It is very hard . . . And it doesn't matter how smart you are. It doesn't matter whether you went to Harvard or Yale or Stanford. Coming and teaching students who are underskilled and who have historically been underserved is really hard work."

Personal Support for Students

The low reading skills of incoming students are not the only challenge that the faculties of New York City's small schools of choice contend with. Another is students' unstable home situations that make it difficult for them to concentrate on academic work. Shannon Curran described a few of these situations. Some SLJ students live in low-income single-parent households, and in some cases an inability to pay the rent requires frequent moves. The range of issues to be addressed in any given year is enormous. One student lived in homeless shelters throughout her tenure at SLJ; some students suffer abuse at home; still others experience violence regularly in their neighborhoods and when traveling to and from school. There are a few students with immigration status issues, making the dream of college even more out of reach—something that does not always get surfaced until senior year. All of these issues compound the already difficult work of serving students needing extra support with their academics.

Finally, since many students enrolled in the small schools of choice do not know anyone who has graduated from college and succeeded in a middle-class job, it is difficult for them to envision that they might do these things. Nor do many students know about financial aid opportunities or the process of applying for aid.

In upper-middle-class families like those of Alexander Williams and Garrett Tallinger (see chapters 2 and 3), parents provide many of the opportunities and supports their adolescent children need to prepare for success after high school, including summer learning opportunities, SAT tutors, college counselors, and visits to colleges. But like Anthony Mears and Harold McAlister, their counterparts in Annette Lareau's study, students attending the NYC schools of choice often live in families that lack the resources to do these things or have parents without any personal experience with college. This means that the schools and their partners must try to do it all. East Side House runs a college preparation and leadership program that prepares Mott Haven Village Prep's students for PSAT and SAT examinations, helps with college and financial aid applications, and assists students in finding paid internships. SLJ and Mott Haven Village Prep students visit several colleges prior to the application process to develop a sense of what "going to college" really means. Guidance counselors at both schools push parents to submit the tax returns needed to apply for federal financial aid. Both schools provide students with summer learning opportunities and employ staff to support them during their college years.

Design Principles

The NYC small schools of choice share common goals and many important design elements, largely because the Request for Proposals for New Century High Schools specified certain common design principles. These included a rigorous instructional program; personal, continuous, and close connections between every student and one or more adults; ongoing assessment of student learning; community involvement in creating extended learning opportunities for students; and student input into the operation and governance of the school. Another contributing factor is the New York State requirement that high school students must pass Regents examinations in five subjects to obtain a Regents diploma. Since 2011, the state has allowed no local alternative to the Regents diploma. Consequently, the Regents exams play a large role in determining the scope and rigor of the curriculum of all public high schools in New York.

Within the common framework, there is wide variation in the themes of the NYC schools of choice, the opportunities offered by schools and their partners, and details like dress codes. For example, the Urban Assembly School for Law and Justice provides a variety of opportunities to learn about the criminal justice system through its many community partners, which, in addition to a leading law firm, include the Red Hook Community Justice Center, the U.S. District Court, the Brooklyn Law School, and the Vera Institute of Justice. East Side House makes internships and summer learning opportunities available to Mott Haven Village Prep students in the many human service programs it offers to residents of the South Bronx. The High School for Contemporary Arts and its partners, which include the Bronx Council on the Arts and the Apollo Theater, provide students with a curriculum rich in connections to the arts and with a variety of opportunities to develop interests in dance, music, film, and other arts.

The variation among the small schools of choice in themes, requirements, and opportunities, all within the context of common goals and common statewide exit examinations, makes sense for two reasons. First, it helps schools to recruit staff members who share a common vision of how to engage students. In Eric Nadelstern's words, "I think the difference is a small group of educators who all come together because they have the same beliefs about how kids learn, have the opportunity to work with a manageable number of students and [are] committed to doing everything in their power to ensure that those kids don't fail to succeed."[12] And second, requiring that students choose among high school alternatives is a first step toward building commitment to their own education—a necessary condition for effective schooling.

CENTRAL OFFICE LEADERSHIP

Starting in 1969, governance of the New York City public schools was placed in the hands of thirty-two community school districts, many of which were plagued by patronage and dissension. Layered on top of the community school districts, which controlled elementary schools, were six districts controlling secondary schools. All of these were overseen by a system-wide chancellor and a large, notoriously cumbersome bureaucracy. Further complications arose from extremely lengthy and detailed contracts with unions that constrained the hiring, transfer, and dismissal of teachers and school administrators. This extraordinarily complex governance structure threatened to push New Century High Schools to the margins of New York City public education. However, this situation changed dramatically just as the first New Century High Schools were opening.

In June 2002, the New York State legislature granted New York Mayor Michael Bloomberg control of the city's public schools. A month later, Bloomberg appointed Joel Klein to serve as schools chancellor. An intense, combative lawyer who had made his reputation heading the U.S. Justice Department's successful prosecution of Microsoft for violating federal antitrust laws, Klein was determined to reform the public schools.

One of his first acts as chancellor was to appoint Michele Cahill as senior counselor for education policy, which signaled his support for the creation of small high schools. Indeed, in October 2002, Klein announced that as part of his Children First comprehensive reform plan, he would replace large comprehensive high schools with two hundred small schools over the course of the next three years. To facilitate this effort, Klein established an Office of New Schools with the mandate to create a system of good schools. The new small high schools, replacing the city's worst-performing high schools in its poorest neighborhoods, would be visible proof that high school education for urban low-income youth could be improved. Kristen Kane, a young Stanford MBA, took over management of the new office, and Eric Nadelstern became its chief academic officer. It was clear that the central administration was interested in learning from the New Century Schools initiative.

In his eight-year tenure as chancellor, Klein brought about a great many changes in New York City's public education system—too many to describe here. Some, however, were vital for the new small high schools of choice because they provided key elements of the system of supports that the schools needed to serve low-income students effectively. One was the introduction of a school accountability system that gave principals unprecedented authority over large parts of their budgets. In return, school leaders were responsible for demonstrating improvement in student outcomes, as measured by scores on reading and mathematics tests and, for high schools, graduation rates. One element of the accountability system was a funding formula that determined how much money each school would receive based on the number of students it served and its percentage of learning disabled students and English language learners.

A second element was a school report card system: each school receives an annual quality rating from A to F, depending on the quality of the school environment and students' academic performance, as well as on improvement in performance; the ratings are then published in a document available online that includes information about each school's strengths and limitations. For the 2011–2012 school year, the Urban Assembly School for Law and Justice received a rating of A and Mott Haven Village Prep a B.

Another initiative was the New York City Leadership Academy, an independent nonprofit organization that, under a contract with the New York City Department of Education, recruits and trains effective school leaders for New York City's high-poverty schools. In addition to a fourteen-month intensive training program, the Leadership Academy also helps new principals build leadership teams, use student assessment results to guide instructional improvement, and construct budgets that support school improvement. As of 2012, one in six principals of New York City public schools was a graduate of the Leadership Academy.[13]

Under a new contract reached with the teacher union in 2005, schools were no longer required to hire teachers who had been displaced from positions in other schools. This change was especially important for small schools committed to building a close-knit learning community and providing all students with close, long-term relationships with teachers.

Klein's strategy to create a system of great schools also included the introduction of a system to match incoming ninth graders to specific schools. Like Jose and Ashanti, all of the city's 80,000 public school eighth graders are required to list, in order of preference, as many as twelve high schools that they would like to attend. The computer-based matching process then assigns each eighth grader to the highest-ranked school that still has openings. As a result, most students attend schools that they have chosen.

Finally, the chancellor supported the creation of intermediaries called School Support Organizations (SSOs) that provide supports tailored to the needs of individual schools. Some of the SSOs are run by nonprofit organizations such as New Visions and the Urban Assembly,[14] others by New York City Department of Education staff. Schools join the SSO that best meets their needs, and they are free to switch SSOs each year. For example, when Flavia Puello Perdomo became principal of Mott Haven Village Prep following the retirement of founding principal Ana Maldonado, she selected a new SSO that provided more support for new principals.

The SSOs do more than provide logistical support to schools; they also help to improve instruction. For example, SLJ chose to participate in a pilot program offered by its SSO, the Urban Assembly, to assess students' readiness to do college work, analyze the data, and use the results to improve instruction. And the Children's First network that Flavia Puello Perdomo chose for Mott Haven Village Prep provides professional development and coaching for teachers focused on such difficult issues as differentiating instruction in core subjects to serve students with varied skills.

Since SSOs rely on the annual fee schools pay for their services, they have incentives to provide packages of supports that schools find valuable. In many respects, the SSOs play roles similar to those of the preK program of the Department of Early Childhood in Boston and the University of Chicago charter management organization. They all provide critical supports to schools.

In sum, the Klein small high schools policy reflected a rare inside-outside strategy. The inside piece included creation of a process for starting small high schools, strong endorsement of their central role, and a system for holding them accountable. The outside piece included reliance on nonprofit intermediary organizations such as New Visions and the Urban Assembly to support the school creation process and provide many of the school supports that small schools need to develop strong educational programs for disadvantaged youth.

THE EVALUATION EVIDENCE

To create, in nine years, more than two hundred small schools that are open to all students is a remarkable accomplishment.[15] It demonstrates that it is indeed possible to make dramatic changes in secondary school education for disadvantaged youths, even in the nation's largest urban school system. This is an important lesson. The critical question, however, is whether the New Century small high schools of choice and those subsequently created by the Klein administration were more successful at serving disadvantaged youths than the large comprehensive high schools they replaced. Fortunately, the foundations supporting the small schools of choice initiative insisted that a rigorous externally conducted evaluation address this question.

MDRC, one of the nation's most respected contract research organizations, undertook an evaluation of students who had applied to one or more of the 123 new small high schools of choice that opened their doors between September 2002 and September 2006.[16] The evaluation was based on data on more than 21,000 students, 93 percent of whom were black or Latino. Of that group, 83 percent came from low-income families, and more than two-thirds entered ninth grade reading below grade level. Similar to the design of the evaluation of the University of Chicago charter school campuses, the MDRC evaluation compared the educational outcomes of students who won and lost lotteries for entry to particular small schools of choice. Outcomes included rates of course completion and high school graduation and performance on state reading and mathematics examinations.[17]

The graduation rate of students attending one of the small schools of choice was more than 7 percentage points higher than the 68 percent graduation rate of students who applied to the same school but were not admitted.[18] This represents a 10 percent increase in the high school graduation rates of students with a wide range of characteristics, including male students of color whose very low graduation rates had proved extremely difficult to influence.

Other indicators of student success show the same pattern. For example, students enrolled in a small school of choice were considerably more likely to complete course work required for graduation on time and to achieve scores on the state Regents English examination that were at least 10 points above the minimum passing score. In summary, small schools of choice had an important positive impact on the quality of high school education provided to thousands of low-income students in New York City. In the last section of this chapter, we place the accomplishments of the New York City small high schools of choice initiative in the context of the educational challenges facing the nation as a whole.

For Jose Rubio, four years at Mott Haven Village Prep led to his graduation in June 2012. Jose was accepted by several community colleges in

New York City, and plans to study psychology at Borough of Manhattan Community College. Ashanti Baker graduated from SLJ that same month. She was accepted by all of the colleges she applied to, a list that included Syracuse, Stonybrook, Hofstra, Wheaton, and Baruch College of the City University of New York. While Ashanti received offers of financial aid from several of the colleges outside of New York City, the cost, net of financial aid, would still have been almost $25,000 per year. For that reason, Ashanti has decided to study economics at Baruch College, where she and her college advisor estimate the cost to be $7,000 per year. When asked what she would tell an eighth grader about SLJ, Ashanti responded, "You're never an outsider, never alone. You never feel afraid to say 'I don't understand.'"

ONGOING CHALLENGES

While New York City's small schools of choice have improved educational opportunities for many low-income students, the schools and the system that supports them face difficult challenges. Most immediately, they need to cope with the consequences of cutbacks in public funding stemming from the severe recession that began in late 2007.[19] One response to the budget cuts at the system level has been to mandate that schools hire teachers already on the NYC payroll rather than allowing schools to hire any licensed teacher. This has made it more difficult for some small schools such as Mott Haven Village Prep, which is located in a relatively dangerous neighborhood, to find skilled teachers who embrace the school's mission. The cutbacks also jeopardize activities such as summer internships, college visits, and the positions of staff dedicated to supporting alumni during their college years. The principals of MHV Prep and SLJ see these activities, which middle-class parents provide to their children, as essential in preparing students to succeed in college.

Declines in funding have also exacerbated a problem that the small schools of choice have faced since their inception: burnout of teachers and school leaders. Like many start-up school ventures dedicated to serving low-income children, SLJ, MHV Prep, and the other small schools of choice intentionally hired dynamic educators eager to go the extra mile to meet students' many needs. The pattern is a familiar one: as young teachers have married and started families, their need for a better balance between the demands of family and work has grown, with many leaving for jobs with lower stress or more manageable hours. Diminished funding, resulting in staffing cuts, places a heavier burden on the staff members who remain, jeopardizing the balance necessary for these educators to continue their important work. Figuring out a way to make the level of work sustainable remains a challenge here.

Another challenge for the New York City schools is to respond constructively to the realization that some students are not well served by "college for all," including students with severe learning disabilities as well as those interested in pursuing a traditional trade—as an electrician or plumber, for example—or a newer occupation such as an electronics technician or marine systems technician. In a promising development, a growing number of small Career and Technical Education high schools have been created that provide the close relationships with teachers that are a hallmark of the city's small schools of choice, but that work with partners to prepare students to enter the work force or postsecondary training programs immediately after high school graduation. This requires balancing the need for a curriculum academically rigorous enough to prepare students for the Regents examinations and to succeed in postsecondary training programs with the need to teach the technical skills students require to be attractive to potential employers.[20]

Finally, it has been a challenge to manage the political problems that arise when failing schools are closed. No matter how poor a school's performance, there is a constituency supporting it, typically including neighborhood parents and alumni and teachers. The magnitude of this problem became evident in 2003 when neighborhood groups came together to protest the closing of Bushwick High School in Brooklyn, a school with a graduation rate below 50 percent, and the problem continues today. There is resistance not only to closing large comprehensive high schools, but also to closing relatively new small schools that either were not able to find a niche or failed to live up to their initial promise. As Eric Nadelstern points out, using scarce resources appropriately means providing schools with autonomy, support, and accountability, and closing those that fail to meet performance standards. As he puts it, "There is no school that would not benefit from this relationship, even if it means . . . within a few years that a school doesn't deserve to exist and should be closed down to give other people an opportunity to do a good job." [21]

THE BIG PICTURE

Most low-income students do not attend high schools that offer the personalized attention, academic rigor and relevance, and abundant learning opportunities that SLJ and MHV Prep provided to Ashanti Baker and Jose Rubio. Indeed, almost two million students in our nation, most from low-income families, attend high schools with graduation rates below 60 percent. [22] Few students attending these high schools will be able to attain the American Dream of upward mobility.

The evidence from the small schools initiative in New York City provides three lessons about improving the life chances of low-income teenagers. The first is that good high schools improve the graduation chances for disadvantaged students, and that it is possible to create a system of good high schools, even in the nation's largest public school system. While the details of effective strategies to create systems of effective high schools will vary from place to place, we see promise in the inside-outside strategy that the Klein administration introduced in New York City. Key elements include:

- A competitive design process that encourages initiative within a framework of common principles
- Attention to best practices for supporting adolescent development
- Important roles for community partners
- A school choice process for students
- Accountability for results
- Intermediary organizations that provide school supports and are responsible to schools

A corollary of this first lesson is that improving high schools for disadvantaged students requires fundamental changes from the operating procedures currently in place in most urban school districts. Indeed, it is striking to contrast the New York City small high school initiative with efforts in many other urban school systems to improve education by creating small high schools, but without making many other changes. With funding from the Gates Foundation, many districts have divided the faculty and students of large comprehensive high schools into three or four groups, assigned a principal to each group, and declared that each group would be a small high school. Given that neither teachers nor students made active decisions to be part of the new small schools, it is not surprising that there were few changes in teachers' and students' daily experiences in school and little impact on students' achievement.[23]

The second lesson is that improving the high school graduation rates of disadvantaged youth by improving high schools is likely to be a good social investment. Using the MDRC finding that the small schools of choice increased the high school graduation rate of low-income students by 7 percentage points, we conservatively estimate that the financial benefit to the public of the New York City small schools initiative exceeded the cost as long as the initiative increased per-pupil costs by no more than $4,460 per year.[24] It seems unlikely that the increase in per-student costs was that high. Moreover, costs should be lower in other districts that can take advantage of lessons derived from the decade-long New York small schools initiative. Consequently, an important part of the effort to improve the life chances of children growing up in low-income families should be to design and implement systems of high schools that are responsive to the developmental needs of adolescents and support the initiatives of talented educators.

The third lesson is that even the ambitious effort to create a system of effective small high schools left one in four disadvantaged New York City youth without a high school diploma. Given the changes in the economy that we describe in chapter 2, the labor market prospects for these youth are dismal indeed. This reinforces the point that investments prior to high school, including those in the kinds of preschool and elementary school initiatives that we have described in the preceding two chapters, are crucial for preventing some of the cognitive deficits and socio-emotional problems seen in the teenage years. So are investments in supporting low-income families, such as the New Hope program featured in the following chapter. Indeed, providing a good high school education to all students would be much less difficult, not to mention less expensive, if every adolescent entered ninth grade prepared to succeed in high school.

8

Programs That
Support Families

YOUNG CHILDREN DEPEND MOST on their families to provide the kinds of secure and stimulating interactions that they need to develop healthy and productive lives. Is there a role for public policies to improve the life chances of children growing up in low-income homes by supporting their families? In chapter 3, we explained that the family learning environments of low- and high-income children are shaped by many factors, including family income. However, we know that factors besides income also matter: children's school readiness and success benefit when they live with both parents, and when the parents are well beyond their teenage years when the children are born, and have themselves completed postsecondary education. Children with fewer siblings to compete for the time, attention, and resources of their parents tend to do better as well.[1]

Few of these demographic factors are amenable to substantial change through public policy. An ambitious recent attempt to promote marriage and strengthen the relationships of low-income couples failed to accomplish either goal.[2] Abstinence-based high school sex education programs have proved effective only when combined with access to contraceptives.[3] And few programs that have attempted to improve the academic or technical skills of young mothers have produced substantial impacts.[4] Even more discouraging is evidence on the general ineffectiveness of programs that attempt to teach good parenting practices before school entry or to increase parents' involvement in the education of their school-age children.[5]

In contrast, family income *is* amenable to change through public policy actions involving the income and payroll tax systems as well as through income-support programs such as Food Stamps, the Earned Income Tax Credit (EITC), and cash payments from the Temporary Assistance for Needy Families Program. The welfare reforms of the 1990s demonstrated that the American public is willing to increase support for low-income families, but only if this is coupled with strong incentives for parents to earn their way out of poverty.[6] To meet the needs of families with children, the challenge is to develop policies that simultaneously reward work, increase parents' economic resources, and help parents balance the competing demands of work and family. One promising program, a work-based intervention known as New Hope, has demonstrated the ability to accomplish these goals and, as a result, to boost the school success of children. We will introduce the New Hope program through the experiences of one of its participants.

THE NEW HOPE PROGRAM

When she first heard about the New Hope program, Inez was a young mother living in a low-income Milwaukee neighborhood.[7] Born in Puerto Rico, Inez had spent most of her childhood in New York City. Although Inez's mother had worked when Inez was very young, the family turned to support from welfare after Inez's mother threw her abusive husband out of the house. But when Inez was sixteen, an automobile accident left her mother unable to care for her children. With nowhere else to go, Inez came to Milwaukee to stay with her father.

Inez's relationship with her father was turbulent, and he kicked her out when she was eighteen. She lived with boyfriends and got pregnant by one of them. Some of her boyfriends and the men they hung out with were dealing drugs and did prison time. Inez readily admits that she was lucky to avoid serious trouble herself. She managed to graduate from high school on time and began working at a number of jobs. But she was grateful for Wisconsin's cash assistance because it enabled her to care for her child during his first year of life.

Although Inez might have appeared headed for a life on welfare, a few minutes' talking with her makes it clear that history would not repeat itself. She never intended to stay on welfare for long: "One year—that was it." An energetic woman who saw work as a central part of her life and brimmed with confidence about her future career, Inez was working at a part-time job in a drugstore while looking for something better when she heard about New Hope at a job fair and decided to give it a try.

New Hope was an experimental program that operated in the mid- to late-1990s in Milwaukee. It was created by a coalition of community activists and business leaders who believed that work was the best route out of poverty. New Hope's offer was simple: if a low-income individual could document working thirty or more hours per week during the prior month, then that person was entitled to an earnings supplement that would bring family income above the poverty line, plus subsidies for health insurance and child care for people who needed them (figure 8.1). These benefits were provided on a sliding scale that declined as family income increased. If a participant was unable to find a job owing, say, to lack of work experience or a criminal record, the program provided opportunities for temporary community service jobs that paid the minimum wage but still entitled that person to program benefits. All participants had access to help from a counselor who provided information about jobs, educational

Figure 8.1   New Hope Program

What New Hope required:
- Proof of thirty or more hours of work per week

What New Hope provided:
- An earnings supplement that raised income above the poverty line
- Subsidized child care
- Subsidized health insurance
- If needed, a temporary community-service job
- Respect and help from New Hope staff

Who was eligible:
- All adult men and women, regardless of family status, with low family incomes and living in Milwaukee's poorest neighborhoods

opportunities, child care, and other community resources in an atmosphere of respect.

Taken together, New Hope offered a variety of benefits from which participants could choose—a feature that allowed families with diverse needs and circumstances to tailor the program to their own unique situations. Like the school-based programs described in earlier chapters, the program combined support (in the form of benefits) and accountability (the work requirement) to achieve its goals.

New Hope is unusual because it was intended as a two-generation program that would help both parents and children. The people who designed the program knew that income—or lack of it—is a significant determinant of children's life chances, and in particular of their educational success. They believed that increasing family income would improve children's material well-being by reducing episodes of food insufficiency, improving housing and neighborhood conditions, and enabling parents to buy books and other beneficial forms of cognitive stimulation for their children. New Hope's child-care subsidies were designed to enable parents to pay for higher-quality child care and participation in afterschool programs. Its health insurance subsidies were designed to increase access to needed services. All of these features, plus New Hope's supportive counselors, were thought likely to improve maternal mental health and parenting, benefiting children directly or indirectly.

The New Hope program is important because evidence from this and several other work-support programs demonstrates that children's school achievement can indeed benefit from helping parents boost their incomes and balance their work and family responsibilities. Because of these impacts, and because of the importance of home life in children's eventual school success, work-support programs like New Hope are a needed complement to the education-based policies we have featured so far.

NEW HOPE AND THE WORLD OF WELFARE REFORM

New Hope was a social contract rather than a welfare program. It was developed during the 1980s and early 1990s when the nation was moving toward a consensus on the moral value of work and self-sufficiency as a key goal of programs for the poor. Increasing awareness of the plight of working-poor families and political pressures to curtail welfare converged in the familiar themes of Bill Clinton's first presidential campaign. Clinton proposed to "end welfare as we know it," which struck a responsive chord in a nation already primed for its message. From a contentious political debate came, in 1996, national welfare reform legislation that ended cash assistance as an entitlement and required almost all recipients to work.[8] By the late 1990s, the number of people receiving cash assistance had plummeted.

At the same time, both federal and state governments were pouring money into programs that would help "make work pay." The federal government enlarged the Earned Income Tax Credit, which supplemented the earnings of low-income workers. The maximum benefit available to a family with two children increased from \$1,384 per year in 1992 to \$5,236 in 2012.[9] Many states began or expanded their own supplemental EITC programs. In the late 1980s and early 1990s, legislation expanded both health insurance, through the Medicaid program, and child-care subsidies to children of working-poor parents outside the welfare system.

Despite these hopeful developments, the system of work supports remained fragmented. State child-care subsidies often required onerous monthly recertification visits that discouraged many low-income working mothers from applying for them. States struggled with the task of converting their welfare offices into "job transition" offices.[10]

New Hope's designers were confident that their program's partnership approach would help families even more. Julie Kerksick, one of New Hope's founders and directors, put it this way: "The social contract is very clear and is framed as both New Hope and the participant bringing something to the table. We are not about assessing them and telling them what they can or can't do. That is the whole premise of most welfare reforms: the individual is something to be acted upon. New Hope's premise is what we can offer you in return for your work effort."

One key "infrastructure" challenge New Hope faced was to provide services to program participants very quickly after they had lined up a full-time job. Another was to select and train project representatives who would explain New Hope's benefits, process claims, and provide job coaching. Kerksick wanted to find representatives who would mirror the goals of the program and adhere to its philosophy, like good teachers who understand and implement a curriculum as designed. Kerksick described the hiring process as follows: "I asked them to just tell me that they've ever helped somebody get a job . . . I didn't care if it was a cousin or a brother or if they did this while working for Milwaukee County . . . This meant they understood how the labor market worked." But Kerksick also wanted her staff to act as counselors rather than social workers when the meetings with participants began to touch on personal problems. As she put it, "I wanted our reps to treat people with respect and compassion but never to confuse this with friendship."

Like many of the teachers and leaders featured in earlier chapters, New Hope representatives were supported in their work but also held accountable for their performance. All went through an extensive training process to learn the program, and there were frequent staff meetings for talking through complications and new developments in the program and community. On the rare occasions when the match between participant and project representative wasn't working out, Kerksick and her staff would intervene to make better arrangements.

NEW HOPE'S IMPACTS

Evidence on New Hope's effectiveness comes from a random-assignment evaluation conducted by the nonprofit policy evaluation firm MDRC.[11] One-half of the 1,357 individuals who applied for the New Hope program were randomly selected to participate in it for three years. The other half formed the comparison group. All lived in Milwaukee's two poorest zip code areas and continued to be eligible for all other federal, state, and local programs (and to be subject to the rules of those programs) during a period of rapidly changing welfare and poverty policies in Wisconsin and across the nation. Both groups enjoyed the fruits of Milwaukee's strong economy in the mid-1990s, and both could claim the increasingly generous federal and state EITC payments that supplemented the earnings of low-income workers.

With work, poverty, and welfare dominating the public debate at the time, evaluators monitored the implementation of the program and used administrative records to track patterns of employment, earnings, and receipt of food stamps and cash assistance. Two, five, and eight years after participants entered the program, surveys of participants, older children, and children's teachers provided additional information about job histories, family changes, economic circumstances, mental health, and child well-being.

For a close-up view of how the program was affecting families, fieldworkers conducted in-depth interviews during three years of periodic family visits to a representative group of forty-four parents and their children. The families were selected at random from both New Hope families and families in the comparison group. Inez was one of these forty-four. Fieldworkers made an average of seven home visits to each family to discuss family life and, for the twenty-two New Hope families, use of program services.

For Inez, New Hope was a resounding success. When she first applied to New Hope, she was working part-time and caring for her only child, Jorge. Although she met New Hope's thirty-hour per week requirement, her wage rate was only six dollars an hour. Shortly after applying to New Hope, she issued her boss an ultimatum: "Give me seven dollars an hour or I'll quit." Despite promising to arrange a raise, her boss never came through, so Inez quit and landed a job at a big specialty retail store.

New Hope was well matched to Inez's strong desire for self-reliance. Not long after entering the program, Inez gave birth to a second child, Martín. Shortly afterward, she paid a special trip to the New Hope office to make sure that the child-care subsidy for the new baby was in place. On the job front, some combination of Inez's energy, positive attitude, good fortune, and success in landing a job in a business with some genuine opportunities for advancement led to a series of promotions and raises, so that four years after New Hope ended, Inez was earning the equivalent of twelve dollars and fifty cents an hour in a salaried position in the company.[12]

Inez's success story is somewhat rosier than that of most New Hope participants. Averaged across the three years of program operation, employment and earnings impacts of New Hope were quite modest.[13] Relative to the control group, rates of employment were about 5 percentage points higher, while annual earnings were about $570 higher (in 2012 dollars). But these overall figures combine average outcomes for very different groups of participants. Some were already working long hours at very low pay when they signed up for the program. They saw the New Hope earnings supplements as a way of cutting back on overtime or second jobs in order to spend more time with their families.[14] Across all participants working full-time when they enrolled (roughly one-third of all participants), the program generally sustained employment, although fewer participants than members of the control group worked more than fifty hours per week. The remaining two-thirds of participants were either not working at all or, like Inez, were working less than full-time when they signed up for the program. New Hope boosted their employment by 7 percentage points and annual earnings by about $1,100. New Hope's community service jobs played an important role in these impacts, although they did not figure into Inez's successes.

Family income rose as well. Among families with young children, poverty rates were dramatically lower for New Hope participants than for those in the comparison group—17 percentage points lower in the first year, 12 points lower in the second and third years, and 8 points lower in the two years after New Hope benefits stopped. Although New Hope failed to eliminate poverty among all of its families, it was clearly more successful at lifting families out of poverty than was the collection of programs available in Wisconsin in the mid-1990s.

More importantly in terms of the concerns of this book, New Hope's greatest success may well have been its positive impact on school achievement and behavior among children. Inez saw the New Hope benefits as enabling her to provide good child care and offer a little financial security. She was diligent about finding educational experiences, good child care, and recreational programs for both of her boys, and she spent her scarce resources on things she thought would be good for them. She also worked to get her children's father to spend time with her two sons and pay child support.

Program evaluation fieldworkers first met her son Jorge in 1998, when Inez was in her third year of New Hope. At the time, Jorge was a small, dark-haired, lively four-year-old with big brown eyes who was attending a Milwaukee public school prekindergarten program. Inez boasted that he was a good student, but sometimes a little too talkative. At a visit two years later, Inez bragged that Jorge was the best student in his first-grade class. As part of New Hope's evaluation, children were given an achievement test, and Jorge's performance was indeed well above the national average.

By the time of fieldworkers' final visits, Jorge had grown into a friendly and articulate ten-year-old. He had just finished fourth grade, earning Bs and Cs and often getting help with his homework in an afterschool program. His achievement test scores were still above the national average. He liked his last teacher, and thought his school was good because the teachers gave enough homework and paid attention to him and his fellow classmates. Jorge seemed to be engaged in school and was doing fairly well academically. Jorge was still vulnerable to many of the same forces that shaped Anthony Mears's bleak future, and only time will tell whether New Hope will lead to a brighter future.

Boys like Jorge were particularly likely to benefit from the New Hope program. In terms of SAT-type scores, teachers ranked the boys in New Hope families 33 points higher in achievement than boys in comparison families after two years of program operation. Teachers also rated the boys in New Hope families much more favorably than boys in control families on "positive social behavior"—obeying rules in school, being admired and well-liked by other students, and being self-reliant. They reported fewer disciplinary problems among boys from New Hope families and less frequent behavior problems—less arguing, disturbing others, social withdrawal, or sadness.

Impacts for girls were smaller and often not statistically significant. The achievement advantage amounted to the equivalent of 12 SAT points. And teachers rated New Hope girls as somewhat more disobedient and aggressive than girls in control families. Some of the larger impact on boys may be explained by the fact that boys had much more to gain from an intervention than did girls. In the in-depth interviews, mothers often said that their boys were vulnerable, and they used any resources they had to counteract negative influences. As one mother said, "It's different for girls. For boys, it's dangerous. [Gangs are] full of older men who want these young ones to do their dirty work. And they'll buy them things and give them money."[15]

Researchers also conducted interviews five years after the end of the program and found that New Hope children outperformed control-group children in terms of school motivation and positive behavior, and that parents were more likely to report positive parenting (better control, fewer discipline problems).[16] New Hope youth were more optimistic about their educational and occupational prospects. A disappointment was that, in contrast to three years earlier, neither teachers nor parents of New Hope children reported fewer behavior problems for them than the teachers and parents of control-group children.[17] This could be a longer-run result of families no longer having access to New Hope's benefits.

Remarkably, New Hope's child impacts were enjoyed by all types of families enrolled in the program.[18] One might have expected only children in the subset of families with the largest gains in family income to benefit the most. Recall, though, that some parents entered the program already working full-time (or more than that) and used the New Hope benefits as a way to cut back on overtime hours and second jobs, even if that meant some reduction in income. For children in these families, impacts were no different from impacts on children in the families with the largest income gains. Attempts to isolate the single component of the program that fueled the beneficial impacts on children proved unsuccessful. It appears that the combination of benefits, available on a voluntary basis in a menu from which participants could choose to suit their particular needs, was the key to New Hope's success.

HOW GENERALIZABLE ARE NEW HOPE'S RESULTS?

The success of New Hope shows that it is possible to improve schooling outcomes for children by supporting the work efforts of their parents. But is New Hope a viable model for a state or national approach to improving the lot of low-income workers and their children? In many respects, this is the same question that arises when innovative educational reforms depend on a charismatic leader or the devotion of a core group of teachers. In the case of New Hope, the program was community-initiated and served fewer than a thousand adults—all of whom had volunteered for it, knowing that it meant working full-time. It operated for a few years in only two Milwaukee neighborhoods in the context of a booming labor market. Even if New Hope could somehow be scaled up to the state or national level, what are the odds that the improvements it fostered at one particular time and place would be replicated? Perhaps most worrisome for generalizing to other settings, it was run by people who were dedicated to its mission and who viewed participants as partners and treated them with respect. Wouldn't this approach to program administration be difficult to implement in city, county, and state bureaucracies?[19]

Encouraging evidence about "going to scale" comes from neighboring Minnesota. While New Hope was operating in Milwaukee, the state of Minnesota was experimenting with its own version of welfare reform. Like New Hope, the Minnesota Family Investment Program (MFIP) sought to alleviate poverty and encourage work by offering earnings supplements and assuring child-care assistance and health care. Like New Hope, it trained staff members to provide information and supports for people striving to take advantage of the program's work-based benefits.[20] More generally, it sought to build up its infrastructure by transforming the culture of the welfare offices from a preoccupation with minimizing application and payment errors to providing comprehensive counseling and other supports that would facilitate transitions to full-time work. And like New Hope, it was evaluated in a rigorous way.

MFIP was also a success. In fact, the improvements it achieved were similar to those found in New Hope: work and earnings increased sharply, and the increases were maintained for the three-year duration of the program. Family income rose, and poverty dropped. Children performed better in school and exhibited fewer behavior problems than children in the AFDC comparison group.[21] Marriage rates increased, and women's reports of domestic abuse dropped.[22]

Center-based child care and preschool appear to be a key reason for the improved outcomes for relatively young children whose families participated in New Hope, MFIP, and similar programs. Although the quality of this care was probably below that provided in Boston's preK classrooms, the fact that children whose families enrolled in any one of these programs spent more time in early childhood centers than children in the relevant comparison group likely contributed to their higher achievement.[23] It is less certain how these programs affected teenagers. In some of the experiments, children who were adolescents when their mothers were assigned to these programs did not fare as well. Even with increased income, these adolescents had slightly lower school achievement and slower progress through school than adolescents in the control-group families. The lower levels of school achievement may be the result of a lack of supervision during parents' working hours. There is also evidence that the adolescents in program-group families were more likely to be caring for younger siblings or to work many hours per week themselves.[24]

COSTS AND BENEFITS

Social programs are worthy investments only if they generate benefits that exceed the costs of running the program. One cost-benefit study put the total administrative costs of running a scaled-up version of a New Hope-type program at about $2,000 per participant.[25] Did New Hope generate benefits worth as much or more? A key potential benefit of New Hope is its boost to the labor market productivity, measured in earnings, of adult participants. The annual earnings advantage of New Hope participants relative to members of the control group amounted to only about $580 per person. Earnings impacts were twice as high for the participants who were not working at the start of New Hope, but the overall productivity estimate of $580 is most appropriate for our program-wide estimate of costs and benefits. Subtracting the earnings gain from the $2,000 cost leaves a net program cost of about $1,420.

Society could also benefit eventually from New Hope's positive impacts on child achievement and behavior, particularly among boys. It is difficult to assign a dollar value to these impacts, but they are clearly important, given that school achievement has been linked to significant earnings gains in adulthood. Moreover, behavioral improvements that reduce crime can generate very large taxpayer benefits.[26] Researchers used these outcomes to project future costs savings. Given that two years after their families enrolled in New Hope, children were judged by their teachers to have considerably higher achievement than children in the control group, researchers calculated that the projected earnings gains (about $1,500 per student) from higher school achievement would cover the annual net cost of the program.[27]

Two years after the end of the program, teachers also reported that relative to control-group boys, boys in the New Hope program exhibited fewer behavior and disciplinary problems and were more compliant and less hyperactive in classrooms, although, as noted above, some of these gains had disappeared three years later. Given the extraordinarily high crime, dropout, and unemployment costs associated with high-risk behaviors of inner-city minority males, if participation in New Hope resulted in one in sixteen boys engaging in fewer risky behaviors, it would pay for the entire taxpayer cost of the New Hope program.[28] New Hope's large impacts on boys' behavior alone might well be more than sufficient to cover all of the taxpayer's costs. Moreover, improvements in boys' classroom behavior also result in improved academic achievement for classmates, another potential social benefit from New Hope.[29]

THE BIG PICTURE

As shown in chapter 3, family income plays an influential role for children's schooling success, as do the mental health of parents and parenting quality. So it is perhaps not surprising that evaluations of New Hope and similar programs have shown that supporting low-income parents' efforts to balance demands of work and family—and providing even just a little more dependable income—can lead to improvements in children's school achievement and behavior. These findings complement studies, also mentioned in chapter 3, showing that increases in the generosity of the Earned Income Tax Credit increase children's school achievement and reduce maternal stress.[30]

The genius of New Hope's design is that it included work supports that were essential for helping participants balance work and family demands—

an income supplement, child-care subsidies, and health insurance subsidies—and provided them to workers and their families in a single package and from a "one-stop" location. It preserved work incentives by providing the benefits only when families could document substantial work effort (30+ weekly hours). Ensuring that New Hope's service bundle was explained clearly and delivered quickly to participants was tricky, but project representatives were well supported in their efforts—and were held accountable.

Under current policy, the various elements of New Hope are available piecemeal from a variety of programs run by the federal government (e.g., the Earned Income Tax Credit) or the states (child-care subsidies, Medicaid). Their scope and generosity vary greatly from one state to another, and they are typically "siloed" into different agencies.[31] New Hope's evaluation compared how families and children fared with New Hope's package approach relative to the collection of piecemeal supports offered by the state of Wisconsin. It showed that children did better with the package approach.

As policy makers consider the kinds of policies that might help to combat the widening educational attainment gap between high- and low-income children, programs such as New Hope and MFIP that provide work supports for adults deserve a place alongside education programs, as does the continuation of proven programs such as the Earned Income Tax Credit. Supporting struggling families is a vital complement to effective preschool and K–12 education in helping to ensure that children growing up in low-income families are able to overtake their parents in terms of both education and earnings.

9

Restoring Opportunity

WHEN WE LAST SAW Garrett Tallinger in chapter 3, he and his family were busy juggling baseball, soccer, swimming, piano, and saxophone—a very full schedule for a fourth grader. Revisited at twenty years old, he has clearly been well served by his childhood experiences, plus the many Advanced Placement and honors courses he took in high school. Garrett is majoring in business at a well-regarded university and looks forward to starting a family of his own. Alexander Williams, after a similarly busy childhood and challenging classes, is also doing well at the age of twenty. He is on his way to medical school. His busy schedule, ample family resources, and constant guidance from his parents and teachers, as described in chapter 2, have propelled him to success in college and, in all likelihood, beyond.

The families of Garrett and Alexander embody the kinds of upward mobility that Americans cherish. Only one of Garrett's grandparents had taken any college courses, but both of his parents have college degrees, and Garrett appears well on his way to completing at least that much education. We have no information about the education of Alexander's grandparents, but all worked in blue-collar or clerical jobs. Alexander's parents hold advanced degrees in business or law, and Alexander plans to become a doctor.

The picture of family life and intergenerational mobility is very different for Harold McAlister and Anthony Mears, the other two subjects of Annette Lareau's study that we describe in chapters 2 and 3. Harold's fourth-grade year was much less structured than Garrett's and Alexander's. It was also constrained by a family budget so tight that Harold and his siblings sometimes went hungry. Harold was a talented basketball player, but a marginal academic record and problems with his coach kept him from a spot on his high school's basketball team. Working as a busboy and then waiter at a local restaurant during high school, Harold dropped out altogether only a few weeks before graduation. Failing to complete high school, Harold fell short of his mother's educational attainment. At age twenty, he's living with his brother, his brother's girlfriend, and their three children, and working as a waiter in that same chain restaurant. He hopes to go back to school "someday."

Like Harold, Anthony Mears is struggling to make ends meet in the low-wage labor market. Like his mother, Anthony completed some college after high school, but he has nothing to show for the $2,500 his parents spent on community college tuition. After a string of low-wage jobs in a shopping mall and a drug store, he is working with his cousin for $12.50 an hour in a construction job. The pay isn't too bad, but the work is unsteady.

These stories are more than interesting anecdotes. They are telling reminders of how quickly children can fall behind, and how much more severe the consequences are today than in the past, when someone like Harold and Anthony who found school "not that interesting" might still expect to find a well-paid job. For many of the nation's young people, the path into the middle class used to be much clearer and more accessible. Today that path is more arduous and dependent on success in school, and the consequences of falling behind are far more severe.

The growing achievement and attainment gaps between children from low- and higher-income families threaten the nation's future. They jeopardize economic growth because a large percentage of children, overwhelmingly from low-income families, end their formal schooling without the skills to earn a decent living in an economy that is rapidly changing as a result of technological advances and globalization. The American Dream of upward socioeconomic mobility is now beyond the reach of many low-income children. This is particularly distressing because a shared belief in upward mobility has always been the glue that holds our diverse, pluralistic democracy together.

It will be extraordinarily difficult to reverse the striking growth in inequality in educational outcomes in the United States, for several related reasons. First, as we discussed in chapter 2, changes in the economy have ratcheted up the skills and educational attainments Americans need to earn a good living. These changes are likely to persist into the foreseeable future. Second, the same computer-based technological changes that make it essential for all children to master more demanding skills have also widened the gap between the opportunities of low-income and higher-income children to acquire these skills. High-income parents, most of whom have college degrees, can invest in their children's education by choosing where to live and which schools their children will attend, and by using their financial resources and knowledge to help their children acquire skills and knowledge beyond what is taught in school. In contrast, low-income parents, most of whom have no postsecondary education, lack the resources to provide for their children's education in the same ways. As explained in chapter 3, the inequality is evident early: low-income children lag well behind children from higher-income families by the time they enter kindergarten. Thus, the same forces that have increased inequality in family incomes perpetuate that inequality and reduce the potential for upward mobility.

Differences in schools serving high- and low-income children reinforce the trend toward greater inequality. As we showed in chapter 4, low-income children are increasingly likely to attend schools serving other children from low-income families, many of whom arrive at school unprepared to contribute to their own education and that of their classmates. High rates of student turnover and the burdens of classmates with learning and behavior problems contribute to the low quality of education in a great many high-poverty schools.[1] So does the difficulty most high-poverty schools experience in attracting and retaining skilled teachers. And teachers in high-poverty schools tend to work in relative isolation under difficult circumstances that hinder the improvement of their teaching skills.[2] As a result, low-income students are unlikely to receive consistently effective, well-coordinated instruction.

Inequality in access to coordinated, excellent instruction is not a new problem in the United States. Indeed, as explained in chapter 4, it has a long history, rooted in local control of public education, teacher contracts that base pay solely on degrees and seniority, and transfer provisions that leave high-poverty schools staffed with a disproportionate number of novice teachers.[3] What is different today from several decades ago is the much greater lifelong cost to students of an inadequate education. Differences in educational quality are now much more likely than in the past to magnify the gap in life outcomes between children from high- and low-income families.

Another obstacle to reversing the growing inequality of educational outcomes is that a great many low-income parents, despite frustration with their own inability to earn a decent living, do not understand that their children will fare better only if they master the difficult conceptual skills laid out in the Common Core standards. Indeed, many parents correctly observe that their children are learning at least as much in school as they did but fail to realize that the more sophisticated skills their children need can only be acquired with different, better instruction. While they may be frustrated by disorder and lack of discipline in their children's schools, they lack the knowledge and experience needed to be strong supporters of instructional changes aimed at preparing students to master the Common Core standards.

DISAPPOINTING RESULTS FROM RECENT IMPROVEMENT STRATEGIES

In the face of these strong economic headwinds, states and the federal government have emphasized two strategies to improve public education over the past several decades. The first, dominant from 1965 through the mid-1980s, was to devote more resources to schools in low-spending communities and those serving large numbers of children from disadvantaged populations. The second, dominant in the past two decades, has been test-based accountability. While the results of these strategies vary among states, overall the results have been disappointing. This has led to calls for new organizational structures, but also to doubts about their promise. We briefly consider these reform approaches in turn, recognizing that each has been the subject of many book-length studies. None has succeeded, we argue, because none has focused on the difficult task of improving instruction in high-poverty schools and providing students with the coordinated learning experiences they need to master critical skills.

More Money

As a result of successful suits filed in state courts on behalf of families in low-spending districts, many states substantially increased funding of public education during the 1970s and 1980s, achieving some success in reducing inequality of expenditures.[4] The federal government also recognized the financial needs of schools serving large numbers of children from low-income families. Passage of the Elementary and Secondary Education Act in 1965 provided compensatory education (Title I) funds to states and local school districts to be channeled to such schools. In fiscal year 2011, Title I compensatory education funds totaled $14.5 billion.

While analysts disagree on some of the consequences of increased school funding, few, if any, believe that it has been effective in closing gaps in educational outcomes between children from low-income and higher-income families. Evidence from evaluations of the Title I program explains why. It is clear, for example, that in most cases each dollar in Title I money received by a local school district increases the district's education expenditures by considerably less than one dollar, since many communities substitute Title I aid for some of the local tax revenues they would otherwise have devoted to public education.[5]

When money does find its way into school budgets, the impact on student achievement is, at best, modest.[6] One reason is that Title I funds are dispersed too widely, with insufficient concentration on schools serving the greatest numbers of low-income children. Moreover, many school leaders use the funds inefficiently—for example, by pulling Title I–eligible children out of class for remedial instruction. While this practice assures compliance with the regulation that Title I funds be spent on eligible children, it often means that children miss out on instruction provided by their primary teacher.[7]

Finally, few school leaders have been adept at guiding efforts to improve teaching, a process that requires opening up classrooms to frequent observation by supervisors, coaches, and peers, and enlisting all teachers and administrators in the effort to improve instruction.[8] Instead, most have used Title I funds to purchase goods and services that have little impact on the work teachers do with students, and consequently, little impact on student achievement. Thus, spending more money in ways that do not alter the organization of schools and the daily work of teachers and students makes little difference to student achievement.

But it would be wrong to conclude that money never matters. The systemic instructional improvements and rich learning experiences that took place in the Boston preK programs, at the University of Chicago Charter School campuses, and at the Urban Assembly School for Law and Justice and other small schools of choice in New York required significant financial resources. In the Boston preK program, these extra resources paid for ongoing high-quality coaching and the fees associated with applying for National Association for the Education of Young Children accreditation. The resources of the University of Chicago's Urban Education Institute paid for in-depth diagnostic reading assessments at the North Kenwood/Oakland campus and for helping the school's teachers learn how to use the results to improve teaching and learning. At SLJ and Mott Haven Village Prep, money, much of it raised through private foundations, paid for summer learning experiences and college trips, activities critical to preparing low-income students to thrive after graduation. So money can make a difference, but only if it is used effectively to improve the quality of instruction and to enrich children's learning experiences.

Test-Based Accountability

Frustrated that simply increasing funding had yielded no dramatic improvements in public education, state policy makers turned to a different improvement strategy in the late 1980s and 1990s: standards-based educational reforms. The basic idea was to specify the skills students should master at each grade level and develop assessments to measure the extent to which children had mastered them. Over time, standards-based reforms morphed into test-based accountability, with the emphasis on holding schools accountable for children's mastery of the skills laid out in state standards.

During the past two decades, almost all states have introduced test-based accountability as the central component of educational reforms. The No Child Left Behind Act (NCLB), which President George W. Bush signed into law in January 2002, made this the dominant theme of the federal government's strategy to improve the nation's public schools. Schools that fail to make adequate yearly progress in increasing the fraction of students who demonstrate proficiency on state tests of English and mathematics skills are subject to sanctions and may be closed. As a result, improving students' performance on the state-mandated tests is a dominant concern in virtually all high-poverty schools.

The compelling logic underlying test-based accountability is that English and mathematical skills predict labor-market success in adulthood.[9] Consequently, it makes sense to push schools to boost children's skills in these domains. However, educators' responses to the new accountability pressures have not always improved educational quality. The best available evidence indicates that NCLB has at best modest positive effects on reading and math scores in some grades, as measured by national tests.[10] More troubling, NCLB has created incentives for states to choose relatively undemanding tests and set low proficiency thresholds. As a result, performance on many state tests fails to provide valid information about students' readiness to succeed in postsecondary education and earn a decent living.[11] Moreover, some schools, particularly those least capable of educating children effectively, have responded to accountability pressures by narrowing the curriculum and neglecting skills and areas of knowledge that may be important in students' subsequent lives but that are not measured by state-mandated tests.[12] Others have focused undue attention on the subset of students scoring quite close to the minimum proficiency standard, neglecting those with weaker skills.[13] An even more troubling response is that some teachers and administrators have manipulated students' test scores.[14]

Because of concerns that NCLB has not consistently resulted in better education, especially in high-poverty schools, many states have requested waivers from some of the accountability provisions. As of this writing, the U.S. Department of Education had authorized thirty-four states to substitute alternative accountability provisions for certain NCLB regulations.[15] It is too soon to know whether the alternative provisions will result in better education for low-income children.

In summary, the accumulating evidence suggests that NCLB fails to provide the kind of well-designed accountability system that American schools need to improve the quality of public education. We do not attempt to detail an alternative accountability system. However, we do explain below what accountability looks like in the Boston preK system, the NKO charter school, and SLJ. More generally, a better accountability system must satisfy at least two conditions. First, it must result in improved incentives for skilled teachers to work in high-poverty schools. Second, it must encourage teachers to work together to provide all students with the wide range of skills they will need to thrive in twenty-first century America.

Different Organizational Structures

Some analysts have suggested that the reason why more money and test-based accountability have not produced markedly better education for low-income children is that a great many school districts, especially those in big cities, are dysfunctional.[16] A possible implication is that changes in organizational structures might be sufficient to improve education. Some see promise in reconfiguring school districts along the lines of what Joel Klein did in New York. As explained in chapter 7, key elements of the Klein reforms included providing individual schools with control over larger parts of their budget and greater flexibility in hiring staff; allowing them to choose a network to provide the supports they needed, such as professional development; and permitting them to purchase such services as art and music instruction from outside organizations. In return for this increased control of resources, schools are responsible for demonstrating improvement in student outcomes.[17]

While advocates see the district reforms that Klein introduced in New York as a promising model for improving public education, critics point out that some cities that adopted at least some of these governance changes have seen little success.[18] They also point to the exceptional circumstances that led to Klein's appointment as school chancellor and argue that in many other urban districts, local politics would prevent widespread adoption of this approach. They remind advocates of school district reforms that the political motivations of local school committee members, the brief tenure of most urban superintendents, and the sclerotic nature of most school district bureaucracies pose enormous obstacles to long-lasting, constructive change in these institutions.[19]

Some critics of existing educational institutions see networks of charter schools, which are public schools freed from some of the regulations that govern conventional public schools, as a more promising organizational reform. In most states, charter schools are concentrated in urban areas and provide significant numbers of low-income families with educational choices. Advocates argue that competition from charter schools has also contributed to constructive changes in school district practices and contracts with teachers' unions.[20] Critics of charter schools counter that charter schools do not compete with conventional public schools on an even playing field. For example, by establishing rigorous codes of student conduct, some charter schools push out students who exhibit behavior problems and disrupt the education of their classmates, thus increasing the share of such students in conventional public schools.[21]

The net effect of charter schools on American public education remains to be seen. Indeed, given that the regulations governing charter schools vary greatly from state to state, the impacts may vary among states as well. What is quite clear at this point, however, is that only a minority of charter schools are more effective at educating low-income students than conventional public schools.[22] As we explain in chapter 6, this is hardly surprising. The task of educating large numbers of low-income children is too difficult for schools to do successfully on their own over the long term.

Just as conventional public schools serving large numbers of low-income children need significant school supports to succeed, so too do charter schools. This explains why a growing number of charter schools are affiliated with a charter management organization. Examples of CMOs include Uncommon Schools, Achievement First, and Green Dot Schools. The success of charter management organizations in providing critical school supports to charter schools in their networks will be a crucial factor in those schools' effectiveness in educating low-income students.

Another group of analysts argues that providing students, especially those from low-income families, with a wider array of educational choices, including private schools, is the only way to improve American education. They point out that affluent parents use their resources to find public or private schools that meet their children's educational needs, and that low-income parents should also have such choices.[23] They advocate for creating publicly funded educational vouchers that parents could use to pay for all or part of the cost of education at participating private schools as well as at public schools. In support of this recommendation, advocates point to innovations like the New York Scholarship Program, which offers scholarships to pay part of the tuition at private schools and appears to have improved test scores for some black children from low-income families.[24]

Critics caution against drawing general conclusions about the consequences of large-scale voucher programs from evaluations of small programs for which only low-income students were eligible. They point out that the adoption of large-scale voucher programs in Chile and New Zealand increased school segregation by family income. In the United States, such income-based school segregation has followed from the growing residential isolation of low-income families and has reduced the quality of education that low-income American children receive.[25]

In summary, the myriad strategies that states and the federal government have adopted to improve public education in the United States have not stemmed the growing gaps in educational outcomes between children from low-income and higher-income families. In part, these strategies have been overwhelmed by more fundamental changes in the environment in which schools operate. Economic forces have led to growing inequality in family incomes and in parents' capacity to provide and advocate for good education for their children. And there is every reason to believe that these economic forces will continue to persist.

But even in the absence of the damage wrought by growing income inequality, we believe that past and current strategies are inadequate to provide most low-income American children with the skills and knowledge they will need in adulthood to support their own children. Key here is that these strategies have not focused on the difficulty of improving instruction in high-poverty schools and providing students with the coordinated learning experiences they need to master critical skills.

BUILDING BLOCKS FOR AN AMERICAN SOLUTION

It is easy to dwell on the characteristics of American education and the growing inequality of children's circumstances, factors that make constructive change difficult. However, America also has formidable strengths, and we must build on those strengths to meet the challenge of providing low-income children with the high-quality education they need to have a shot at the American Dream of upward mobility. Some longstanding strengths lie in values and commitments. Americans across the political spectrum embrace, at least rhetorically, the value of equality of opportunity and a commitment to education as the primary social institution for achieving that goal. While there are sharp disagreements on the best way to improve education for children from low-income homes, most Americans accept that doing so is an important societal objective.

Other, more recent strengths are derived from a better understanding of how to improve the life chances of low-income children. They include widespread acceptance of the Common Core State Standards; lessons about the critical role of school supports; growing appreciation of the need for well-designed accountability; advances in knowledge about the components of good preK, elementary school, and high school education; and growing evidence on the benefits to children of supporting low-income families. Together, these constitute the building blocks for making real progress in improving the life chances of low-income children. We consider these in turn.

The Common Core State Standards

The Common Core Standards outline the skills in English language arts and mathematics that American students are expected to master at each grade level from kindergarten through twelfth grade. As of this writing, forty-five of the country's fifty states have adopted these standards, which set goals that are considerably higher than the accomplishments of most American students, especially those from low-income families. Figure 9.1 lists some of the Common Core standards in reading, writing, and mathematics for third grade.[26]

Creating the Common Core Standards in English language arts and mathematics is an important step in preparing American students to thrive in a rapidly changing economy and society. Carefully designed to reflect the latest research, the standards can offer teachers and school leaders a fundamental school support: clarity about the conceptual and procedural skills children should master in each grade. And the assessments that two consortia of states are developing to measure students' mastery of the Common Core Standards can provide another critical school support: detailed information for teachers about children's mastery of essential skills and knowledge. These are remarkable accomplishments, reflecting a level of rigor and a degree of cooperation among states that few observers of American education would have thought possible thirty years ago.

Of course, common standards and high-quality assessments alone do not produce better teaching, nor do they enhance student learning. Indeed, the Common Core State Standards represent only an early step down a long path leading to better education for all American children. Yet clarity about the specific skills students should master at each grade level makes it possible to improve teacher training programs and on-the-job professional development. The standards can also facilitate the development of curricula and assessments that are closely aligned with their content. Better teacher preparation and better curricula are essential elements for improving teaching and learning.

Supports and Support Organizations

Preparing large numbers of low-income children to meet demanding academic standards is extremely difficult work. Most schools serving low-income students lack the human resources and the knowledge to do this work successfully without strong supports. The schools we described in chapters 5 through 7 have these supports in place. Shannon Keys took a pay cut to join the NKO faculty because she saw that the school had

Figure 9.1   Common Core third-grade academic standards

ENGLISH LANGUAGE ARTS

Reading standards for literature	Reading standards for informational text	Writing standards
Recount stories, including fables, folktales, and myths from diverse cultures; determine the central message, lesson, or moral and explain how it is conveyed through key details in the text.	Describe the relationship between a series of historical events, scientific ideas or concepts, or steps in technical procedures in a text, using language that pertains to time, sequence, and cause/effect.	Write informative/explanatory texts to examine a topic and convey ideas and information clearly. a. Introduce a topic and group related information together; include illustrations when useful to aiding comprehension. b. Develop the topic with facts, definitions, and details. c. Use linking words and phrases (e.g., also, another, and, more, but) to connect ideas within categories of information. d. Provide a concluding statement or section.

MATH

Operations and algebraic thinking	Number and operations	Measurement and data
• Represent and solve problems involving multiplication and division. • Understand properties of multiplication and the relationship between multiplication and division. • Multiply and divide within 100. • Solve problems involving the four operations, and identify and explain patterns in arithmetic.	• Use place value understanding and properties of operations to perform multi-digit arithmetic. • Develop understanding of fractions as numbers.	• Solve problems involving measurement and estimation of intervals of time, liquid volumes, and masses of objects. • Represent and interpret data. • Geometric measurement: understand concepts of area and relate area to multiplication and to addition. • Geometric measurement: recognize perimeter as an attribute of plane figures and distinguish between linear and area measures.

Source: Common Core State Standards Initiative, www.corestandards.org.

access to the kinds of supports needed for success: one-on-one coaching in implementing a balanced literacy curriculum, student assessments to help guide instruction, and time during the school day to collaborate with and learn from other teachers. Jason Sachs and his colleagues in the Department of Early Childhood organized the training and one-on-one coaching, offered by skilled professionals such as Marina Boni, that Boston's preK teachers needed to teach the rich English language arts and mathematics curriculum effectively. The Urban Assembly provides coaching to SLJ faculty on how to administer a college-readiness assessment and make constructive use of the results. Mott Haven Village Prep's lead community partner, East Side House, provides important learning opportunities for students outside the school setting, as do SLJ's many partners.

As explained in chapter 4, promoting high-quality education for low-income children requires institutions that provide supports of the same high quality as those afforded to NKO and the other schools we have highlighted. Although the United States has yet to develop an adequate set of institutions that do this effectively, a promising recent trend is the growing number of organizations that offer supports to public schools. Some, like the New York Leadership Academy and New Leaders for New Schools, prepare principals to create schools that are effective learning communities for both teachers and students. Others, like Teach for America and the Boston Teachers Residency Program, recruit academically talented college graduates and support their work in high-poverty schools. Still others, like New Visions for Public Schools, the Urban Assembly, and many charter management organizations, recruit leadership teams to start new schools and provide ongoing support for those teams. And then there are the comprehensive school reform design organizations such as Success for All that offer detailed guidance and tools to large numbers of high-poverty schools. The challenge is to devise organizational structures that provide high-poverty schools with the resources, knowledge, and freedom to choose the collection of supports they need.

Accountability

Over the last twenty years, it has come to be almost universally accepted that schools should be judged by their effectiveness in educating students—an enormously important change in thinking. A well-designed accountability system promotes a willingness to use resources in new ways and offers incentives for school faculties to work together to develop the skills of every student. All of the schools introduced in chapters 5–7 face accountability pressures. For the elementary schools participating in the Boston preK programs, accountability came in the form of the expectation that each school would obtain and retain accreditation from the National Association for the Education of Young Children. For the University of Chicago charter schools and the small schools of choice in New York City, accountability included the requirement that their students score well on state-mandated examinations.

In all of the schools we described in chapters 5–7, teachers and school leaders experience a more immediate and more important type of accountability: a responsibility to their colleagues for educating every student. For Boston preK teachers, it included taking advantage of the coaching that Marina Boni and her colleagues provided. For the teachers at NKO, it included working together to make implementation of the balanced literacy curriculum more consistent. For the ninth-grade teachers at SLJ, it meant embracing their shared responsibility to develop the skills of all incoming students, including those reading far below grade level.

As the mounting evidence on the weak effects of No Child Left Behind illustrates, it is extraordinarily difficult to design accountability systems that take into account the intense challenges of educating high concentrations of low-income children and at the same time provide incentives for educators to work together to serve all students well. There will be much to learn from the alternative accountability systems put in place by states that have been granted NCLB waivers. It will be even more important to monitor and learn from the experiences of states as they incorporate student results on new Common Core–based assessments into accountability systems.

We caution against letting high-stakes accountability get ahead of the difficult work of providing educators in high-poverty schools with the knowledge and extensive school supports they will need to help their students master the Common Core Standards. Only if consistent, strong supports are in place can accountability improve the education of low-income children. In other words, strong supports and well-designed accountability are essential complements, not substitutes. Moreover, accountability that improves education in high-poverty schools must encourage and not undercut the shared work that allowed the Boston preK program, NKO, SLJ, and Mott Haven Village Prep to serve low-income students much more effectively than most high-poverty schools do.

Advances in Knowledge

Increased understanding of children's developmental needs, as well as advances in administrative data systems and research designs, have expanded the knowledge available to educators about how to serve children well. Indeed, insights from research informed the design of the school initiatives we highlighted in previous chapters, and they have the potential to benefit other high-poverty schools as well. Jason Sachs and his colleagues, for example, were motivated by recent research findings to focus on developing children's language, mathematics, and socio-emotional skills and to select curricula that allowed children to develop these skills through hands-on exploration and group interactions. Indeed, Boston was able to take advantage of lessons learned from the rigorous evaluations of a growing number of preschool curricula that have been supported by funding from several federal government agencies and private foundations.[27]

The principals of NKO and the other University of Chicago Charter School campuses were aware of the research showing that a lack of vocabulary and background knowledge prevent many low-income children from comprehending texts in core subject areas such as science and social studies. This led them to adopt curricula and pedagogical strategies aimed at building children's knowledge and vocabulary from the start of kindergarten.[28] They also knew about research showing that effective professional development is a process, not an event; that it focuses on methods for teaching particular skills; that observing effective instruction should be part of the learning process; and that it is important for novices to observe effective instruction and receive detailed feedback on the strengths and weaknesses of their own teaching.

Michele Cahill and Bob Hughes incorporated their knowledge of adolescent development and the skills young people need into the requirements for the proposals they solicited for New York City's new small high schools.[29] For example, the requirement that every small school of choice have community partners was based on an understanding that adolescents need exposure to a variety of role models and opportunities to do authentic work.

The SLJ strategy to develop the literacy skills of incoming ninth graders was based on knowledge that the skills needed for science literacy are different from those needed for literacy in social studies. As a result, teaching literacy skills must be at the center of the work of all faculty members, not just English teachers. The faculties of Mott Haven Village Prep and SLJ knew about the research on "summer melt," the phenomenon that many low-income students graduate from high school intending to enroll in college the next fall, but do not follow through because of the complexity of the financial aid application process and fear of the unknown.[30] As a result, both schools developed strategies to support recent graduates during the period of transition to college.

In the case of the New Hope work support experiment, program designers were able to take advantage of research that identified the best ways of integrating benefits into a seamless bundle while avoiding the work-disincentive effects that arise when benefits are "phased out" as earnings rise.[31] These are just a few of the examples of the many ways that advances in knowledge have provided educators and other service providers with better tools to serve the needs of low-income children.

Supporting Families in Ways That Help Children

Families are the most important influence on children's development, but macroeconomic changes over the past several decades have made it harder and harder for low-income parents to provide the kind of learning opportunities for their children that high-income parents provide for theirs. The numbers are sobering: as we saw in chapters 2 and 3, the gap between the family incomes of children at the 20th and 80th percentile of the income distribution grew by $35,000 in the last forty years, and the gap in family expenditures on child enrichment grew by $5,000. No amount of tax reform or increased spending on programs such as the Earned Income Tax

Credit or the Supplemental Nutrition Assistance Program (formerly Food Stamps) can close that kind of gap.

Yet, in a climate of budget cutting and high unemployment, it is important to remind ourselves of the evaluation evidence discussed in chapter 8 showing that a number of family work-support programs that increased family income also boosted the school achievement of younger children. Reductions in the generosity of these kinds of programs would likely reduce the achievement of low-income children. Programs such as the Earned Income Tax Credit developed from a bipartisan belief in the importance of supporting work; research suggests that they have promoted the school success of low-income children and reduced the stress experienced by their mothers.

New Hope's integrated package of work supports was tested against the piecemeal system of programs that Wisconsin offered in the middle 1990s. Its evaluation showed that teachers reported both higher achievement and more positive behavior among New Hope children than children in the comparison group, which suggests the potential value of integrating some of the programs and services that currently support low-income working families. Above all, the evidence from New Hope and other work-support programs shows that they can play a significant role in promoting the learning and social development of low-income children.

MEETING THE CHALLENGE

Historically, the United States has relied on its public schools to solve difficult social problems. For much of the nineteenth and early twentieth centuries, the public schools successfully socialized waves of immigrants to participate in civic life in a pluralist democracy.[32] During the first three-quarters of the twentieth century, schools successfully taught generations of students the basic reading and mathematical skills needed to do the large number of assembly-line and back-office clerical jobs that the economy was producing.[33] Can the nation's schools meet the current challenge of providing all students with the skills they will need to thrive in a rapidly changing economy and society?

It is an enormous challenge. Preparing all students to meet higher academic standards will require instruction that is different and much better than the instruction most of the nation's students receive today. And, as a result of improvements in career opportunities for women and minorities, the schools must compete for talented college graduates to a much greater extent than they did four decades ago. Growing inequality in family incomes has resulted in increasing segregation of poor children and middle-class children in different schools. Through a variety of mechanisms described in this book, the increased segregation of schools by income reduces the quality of education provided to children from low-income families. For all of these reasons, simply asking teachers to work harder in schools as they are currently organized will not do the job.

Nor can the challenge be met by the heroic efforts of charismatic leaders who create schools that "beat the odds." They do this in part by devoting vast amounts of time to recruiting teachers who share their vision and are willing to work very long hours creating curricula, offering extra instruction, and providing emotional support to students from troubled homes. The efforts of such educators are laudable and are the subjects of many heartwarming media stories. However, all too often, the successes of such schools are short-lived, as leaders move on and teachers burn out.[34] Meeting the educational needs of low-income students must be done by creating the conditions for systems of effective schools rather than by relying on exceptions.

As noted above, research conducted in recent years provides insights about the education low-income children will need if they are to master higher academic standards. It will take well-educated teachers with deep subject-matter knowledge who are committed to working together to improve instruction and make it more coordinated and consistent. It will take school leaders able to create a culture in which continuous improvement is the norm. It will take access to expertise of a variety of kinds, including the ability to identify children's skill difficulties, to improve instruction, to create and enforce norms for student conduct, and to deal with emotionally troubled children whose behavior disrupts classrooms.

The experiences of high-poverty schools that have made progress in educating low-income children—like many of those profiled in this book—

indicate that it takes more than simply providing good instruction for six hours per day.[35] Typically the school day starts early in these schools, usually with breakfast for the children. It continues until late in the afternoon, providing time for remediation of lagging skills and exposure to enrichment activities. Many of these schools offer instruction on Saturdays and well into the summer months. Unlike typical afterschool and summer programs that do not improve student outcomes because they are disconnected from the core instructional program, the extended-day and extended-year programs in effective high-poverty schools are well-integrated parts of a coherent strategy to continually build children's skills. Another benefit of such a comprehensive approach to schooling is that the school becomes the center of children's daily experiences, which reduces their exposure to the lures and dangers of the neighborhood. The argument that schools can, on a sustained basis, significantly improve life chances for large numbers of low-income children requires this broad definition of schooling.

When teachers and administrators in individual schools try to do this work alone, many become exhausted both physically and emotionally and leave their schools. This explains the fleeting nature of the success of many high-poverty schools. So the challenge is to provide schools with the supports they need to do this work over the long term.

A number of recent studies show that high staff turnover in high-poverty schools does not stem from teachers' reluctance to teach students from low-income families and students of color. Instead, teachers leave high-poverty schools primarily because of poor social conditions for their work. In other words, the school lacks the strong leadership, culture of collaboration and shared responsibility, or resources needed for success.[36] While strong school supports are not a guarantee that high-poverty schools will develop the social conditions required to attract and retain strong teachers, they are a necessary condition. School supports enable schools to become organizations where talented, committed educators want to work, where learning from one another is a daily part of the job, where the adults have the tools to serve children well, and where there are a variety of opportunities to share leadership tasks.

It's important to acknowledge that many elements that research has identified as valuable in strengthening education for disadvantaged students do cost money, including better initial preparation and ongoing professional development for teachers, more opportunities for teachers to work with and learn from one another, higher quality examinations to provide more feedback to both teachers and students, and better pay for teachers who are asked to work hard in especially challenging conditions.

There is ample evidence that simply spending more money is not an adequate strategy for educational improvement. However, it's one thing to acknowledge that money is not a magic bullet for improving schools. It is very different to assert that meaningful improvement in the education of disadvantaged students can (or must) be achieved without significant and sustained expenditure of additional resources on schooling. These expenditures, appropriately targeted and carefully assessed, represent an essential investment in the nation's future.

We return to the question of what schools can accomplish. The answer depends on the nation's commitment to supporting a broad and comprehensive definition of schooling, its recognition of the immense challenges high-poverty schools face, and its willingness to find ways to provide the consistently strong school supports and well-designed accountability necessary for lasting success.

The United States overcame myriad challenges to create and maintain an education system that was the envy of the world for the better part of the last two centuries. In the nineteenth century, the United States was a leader in providing universal primary schooling, and this accomplishment was followed by a dramatic increase in the percentage of young people who completed high school.[37] It also expanded its system of public universities and community colleges to enable millions of students to acquire advanced skills.[38]

In the last four decades, technological change and globalization have created huge new challenges for our country as we seek to continue to provide opportunities for economic mobility for all children. Once again, the nation is turning to its public schools for answers, and the stakes could not be higher.

We have learned a great deal about the building blocks for success in reforming the nation's schools. The challenge that faces us is to combine these elements into structures that provide consistently high-quality education to low-income students. Real progress will require time for experimentation—and evaluation. One sign of success will be the extent to which high-poverty schools are able to attract and retain well-educated, effective teachers. If high-poverty schools are to succeed in improving the life chances of low-income children, the conditions need to be in place for skilled school leaders and teachers to work together on a long-term basis. We can also learn a lot by tracking student scores on tests that are well aligned with the Common Core Standards and by monitoring the high school graduation, college enrollment, and college graduation rates of disadvantaged students. The long-term measure of success will be the educational attainments and earnings of adults who grew up in low-income families and the restoration of intergenerational mobility.

Our nation faces a daunting challenge, and there are many reasons to temper optimism with caution. But given our country's history of innovative responses to difficult social problems, we are convinced that, together, we have the ability to overcome this huge threat to the nation's future.

Notes

Chapter 1

1. Claudia D. Goldin and Lawrence F. Katz, in *The Race Between Education and Technology* (Cambridge, MA: Belknap Press of Harvard University Press, 2008), provide a comprehensive analysis of changes in education, technology, wages, and economic growth across the 20th century. Our account of these trends is summarized briefly in this chapter and detailed in chapters 2 and 3.

2. We draw the cases of Anthony, Alexander, Garrett, and Harold from Annette Lareau, *Unequal Childhoods: Class, Race, and Family Life*, 2nd ed. with an Update a Decade Later (Berkeley: University of California Press, 2011). A sociologist, Lareau sought to understand the family and school dynamics behind children's successes and failures by studying a number of white and African American fourth graders in affluent, working class, and poor neighborhoods. Most of this data collection took place in 1993 and 1994. She also interviewed the boys in 2003 and 2004 at age 20. Anthony Mears is a pseudonym that we use for the boy to whom Lareau gave the name Tyrec Taylor. Lareau also adopts the convention of specifying details of the lives and locations of her children and parents in ways that preserve anonymity.

Chapter 2

1. In 2012 dollars, $200 translates into more than $1,000. We convert all dollar figures to 2012 dollars using the Consumer Price Index for All Urban Consumers (CPI-U). Hewlett-Packard launched the world's first handheld scientific calculator in 1972 and priced it at $395. It was sophisticated enough (and the spaceship's computer elementary enough) to serve as a backup computer for astronauts on some of the Apollo manned space flights.

2. Richard Layard, "Youth Unemployment in Britain and the United States Compared," in *The Youth Labor Market Problem: Its Nature, Causes, and Consequences*, eds. Richard B. Freeman and David A. Wise (Chicago: University of Chicago Press, 1982), 499–542.

3. David H. Autor, Lawrence F. Katz, and Melissa S. Kearney, "Trends in U.S. Wage Inequality: Revising the Revisionists," *Review of Economics and Statistics* 90, no. 2 (May 2008): 300–323. Figure 6A provides information on wage gaps over time for college and high school graduates with 0–9 years of work experience.

4. Richard B. Freeman, *The Overeducated American* (New York: Academic Press, 1976).
5. Background information on the National Longitudinal Study of the Class of 1972 is available at http://nces.ed.gov/pubs94/data/1994487/README.txt.
6. Some 34.5% graduated from high school on time and had not enrolled in 2- or 4-year colleges by 1979. Many of the rest went on to complete one or two years of community college or technical training, sometimes years after graduating from high school.
7. Only 7% of youth stopping with high school degrees had parents with college degrees.
8. "Full-time work" is defined as working 35 or more hours in an average week and, during 1978, spending fewer than 10 weeks laid off or otherwise out of work. Some 64.1% of the high school–only grads worked as craftsmen, operatives, or transport equipment operators. An additional 5% worked as laborers. As was generally the case in the 1970s, the labor force activity of women was much less than that of men. Current-dollar earnings for high school graduate–only men who worked full-time were $12,969. Median earnings for all full-time working men as of March 1978 were $12,465 (Statistical Abstract of the United States, 1979, Table 690, p. 417).
9. Figure 2.1 is drawn from figure 1.4 in Claudia D. Goldin and Lawrence F. Katz, *The Race Between Education and Technology* (Cambridge, MA: Belknap Press of Harvard University Press, 2008), 20. Those authors kindly made their data available to us. Completed schooling is estimated at age 35. We have chosen to use age 14 as a reference point for describing these trends since age 14 reflects an age when adolescents and their parents are starting to firm up their ideas and plans for completed schooling. We could have easily used birth year or age 35 and shifted the calendar-year scale accordingly.
10. It is important to distinguish between mobility within and across generations. The former is often called *intra*generational mobility and refers to changes in the economic well-being of individuals over their lifetimes. The latter—*inter*generational mobility—is the subject of this book. It refers to the extent to which individuals are more likely to fare better economically than their parents. Of particular importance is the question of whether intergenerational upward economic mobility of Americans is as great today as it was in the past.
11. David H. Autor and David Dorn, "The Growth of Low-Skill Service Jobs and the Polarization of the U.S. Labor Market," *American Economic Review* 103, no. 5 (2013):1553–1597.
12. As described in Chapter 1, we draw the cases described in this chapter and in chapter 3 from Annette Lareau, *Unequal Childhoods : Class, Race, and Family Life*, 2nd ed. with an Update a Decade Later (Berkeley: University of California Press, 2011).
13. Alexander Williams, also a pseudonym, is the name of another child studied by Lareau (2011).
14. We thank David Autor for providing these tabulations from the Current Population Survey. Between 1979 and 2009, adult employment in the U.S. grew by 49%. While the share of the employed labor force working in blue-collar jobs declined markedly over this period (from 32% to 20%), the number of workers employed in blue-collar jobs declined by approximately 7%. We define blue-collar jobs as including two major occupational categories. The first includes operators, fabricators, and laborers. The second includes production, craft, and repair workers.
15. Autor and Dorn, "Growth of Low-Skill Service Jobs."
16. U.S. Bureau of Labor Statistics, *Occupational Outlook Handbook*, 1976–1977 ed. (Washington, D.C.: U.S. Department of Labor, Bureau of Labor Statistics, Division of Occupational Outlook, 1976).

17. U.S. Bureau of Labor Statistics, *Occupational Outlook Handbook*, 2000–2001 ed. (Washington, D.C.: U.S. Department of Labor, Bureau of Labor Statistics, Division of Occupational Outlook, 2000).

18. Thomas Lemieux, "The Changing Nature of Wage Inequality," *Journal of Population Economics* 21, no. 1 (Jan. 2008).

19. Autor, Katz, and Kearney, "Trends in U.S. Wage Inequality." The declining value of the minimum wage and the decline in union representation are not independent of technical change and globalization, since these latter forces weakened the political and bargaining power of unions.

20. Ibid., Table 1. Data are based on weekly earnings for full-time male workers with five years of experience. Earnings of high school dropouts fell even more than the earnings of high school graduates (see Frank Levy and Richard J. Murnane, *The New Division of Labor: How Computers Are Creating the Next Labor Market* (Princeton, NJ: Princeton University Press, 2004). In contrast, the earnings of workers at the very top of the earnings distribution soared, the likely result of changing norms for appropriate executive compensation. See Frank Levy and Peter Temin, "Institutions and Wages in Post–World War II America," in *Labor in the Era of Globalization*, eds. Clair Brown, Barry J. Eichengreen, and Michael Reich (New York: Cambridge University Press, 2010), 15–50.

21. As reported by the College Board, the annual price expressed in 2011 dollars increased from $7,079 for the 1981–1982 academic year to $17,131 for the 2011–2012 academic year. Financial aid lessened the financial burden of college attendance for many students from low-income families. But even net of financial aid, college became increasingly unaffordable for many low-income families.

22. According to data collected as part of the National Postsecondary Student Aid Study (NPSAS) and reported in the College Board's document, Trends in College Pricing 2011, the net cost of attendance at a public community college has not increased over the last two decades for students from very low income families who take advantage of all available aid. The reason is that the size of Pell grants has increased as rapidly as tuitions and fees at these institutions. The cost of enrollment in a public 4-year college has increased for students from very low income families because grants have not kept up with the increase in living costs. It is important to keep in mind that applying for federal Pell grants to pay for college is an arduous process that deters many potentially eligible students. Documentation of this is provided by Eric Bettinger et al., "The Role of Application Assistance and Information in College Decisions: Results from the H&R Block FAFSA Experiment," *Quarterly Journal of Economics* 127, no. 3 (2012). The decline in public funding per student for public postsecondary institutions has also contributed to the slowdown in the rate of college completion. One mechanism is an increase in fees. A second is a decline in the number of courses and services offered, especially in public colleges that are not the flagship campuses of state universities. This has made it more difficult for students to complete academic programs required for degrees. See John Bound, Michael F. Lovenheim. and Sarah Turner, "Understanding the Increased Time to the Baccalaureate Degree," *Education Finance and Policy* (forthcoming) for a discussion of factors that contributed to the slowdown in the U.S. rate of college completion, including the decline in public per-student funding of public colleges and universities.

23. Details on the test scores are provided in the text and online appendix of Sean F. Reardon, "The Widening Academic Achievement Gap Between the Rich and the Poor: New Evidence

and Possible Explanations," in *Whither Opportunity? Rising Inequality, Schools, and Children's Life Chances*, eds. Greg J. Duncan and Richard J. Murnane (New York: Russell Sage Foundation and the Spencer Foundation, 2011), 91–116. Reardon analyzes data from 19 different U.S.-based national studies of children's achievement test scores. Although the data are drawn from school children of different ages, he shows that the test-score trajectories of high- and low-income children in the longitudinal data sets are roughly parallel. All of the studies included data on the family incomes of the students taking the tests. Reardon uses the 10th and 90th percentiles of the family income distribution to define low and high incomes. To estimate test score gaps between 90th- and 10th-percentile children, Reardon fits a cubic function of test scores on income within each data set and then interpolates standardized test scores at these two points in the distribution. He then fits quartic trend lines to all of the 90th/10th test score gaps generated by his 19 data sets. To track test scores of children at the middle of the income distribution between 1978 and 2008, we use average reading scores from the National Assessment of Educational Progress (NAEP), which are comparable from one year to the next. We then calculate trends in the reading proficiency of students at the 10th and 90th percentiles of the income distribution by applying Reardon's data on trends in these gaps to the trends in average NAEP scores between 1978 and 2008.

24. Information on average math and reading gains per year of school are provided in Carolyn J. Hill et al., "Empirical Benchmarks for Interpreting Effect Sizes in Research," *Child Development Perspectives* 2, no. 3 (2008): 172–177.

25. The income-based reading gap grew by 33 points across this same period. Readers familiar with trends in the black-white test-score gap may be surprised by this steady widening of the gap, since racial gaps in test scores have diminished considerably in the 50 years since *Brown v. Board of Education*—see Katherine A. Magnuson and Jane Waldfogel, *Steady Gains and Stalled Progress: Inequality and the Black-White Test Score Gap* (New York: Russell Sage Foundation, 2008).Blacks attending school early in the period had very low test scores—some 50 points lower than the larger group of students with very low family incomes. School desegregation eliminated much of the gap between blacks and all low-income students by the mid-1980s, and further growth after 2000 pushed black scores above those of low-income students—see Jonathan Guryan, "Desegregation and Black Dropout Rates," *American Economic Review* 94, no. 4 (Sept. 2004). So while black students gained considerable ground relative to more affluent students, the more general group of low-income children fell further and further behind.

26. The college completion data come from Martha J. Bailey and Susan M. Dynarski, "Inequality in Postsecondary Education," in *Whither Opportunity?*, eds. Duncan and Murnane (2011), and reflect whether individuals had reported completing four years of college by age 25. The data are based on a comparison of the top and bottom income quartiles (25%) of their respective birth cohorts, which is a slightly different way of categorizing income than the 10th and 90th percentiles used in the Reardon (2011) analysis. In percentage terms, the increase from 5% to 9% in low-income children's college graduation rates is larger than the increase from 36% to 54% in high-income children's rates. However, we believe that the absolute changes are more relevant here, with the changes presented in figure 2.3 translating into 4.5 times as many additional college degrees for high-income as compared with low-income children. Duncan and Murnane (2011) find a growing gap in the average number of years of schooling completed by children growing up in high- and low-income families as defined by the top and bottom quintiles of the income distribution. The increase

in the gap—roughly one more year of completed schooling—is comparable to the increase in the test score gap Reardon found. These results are based on data from the Panel Study of Income Dynamics on children turning 14 between 1969 and 1997 and do not count GEDs as added years of schooling.

27. James J. Heckman and Alan B. Krueger, *Inequality in America: What Role for Human Capital Policies?* (Cambridge, MA: MIT Press, 2005).

28. As noted above, the college graduation rates from Bailey and Dynarski (2011) compared the top and bottom 25% of the population. As of 2011, there were about 73.7 million individuals under the age of 18 living in the United States, so each quartile contains about 18.4 million children. Most of the rest of the income-based data presented in the book compare children in the top and bottom 20% of the population ranked by income.

29. Roughly speaking, gross national product (GDP) per capita increased by 75% between 1947 and 1970, as did the incomes of families at the 20th, 80th, and 95th percentiles of the family income distribution (see http://www.census.gov/hhes/www/income/data/historical/families/). Of course, some families had far greater financial resources than others to care for their children. In 1947, the income of families at the 80th percentile of the income distribution was 3.1 times that of families at the 20th percentile; by 1970 the corresponding ratio was virtually identical—3.0 times that of families at the 20th percentile.

30. These income figures are in 2012 dollars and are drawn from the Current Population Survey. We are grateful to Sean Reardon and Demetra Kalogrides for supplying these data. With the cost of living increasing nearly sixfold between 1970 and 2011, the actual (uninflated) family income separating the bottom fifth and top four-fifths of children in 1970 was $6,407. It is important to note that the bar graphs in figure 2.4 provide information for children age 5–17 rather than families or even all families with children. Trends in family-based income differ somewhat from trends in child-based family income. For example, while figure 2.4 shows that the child-based inflation-adjusted family income at the 20th percentile decreased by more than 25% between 1970 and 2011, family-based income increased slightly (by 3%)—see http://www.census.gov/hhes/www/income/data/historical/families/.

31. According to the Current Population Survey, in 2011, 33.6% of children in the bottom fifth of the income distribution had at least one working parent. Some 56.9% of the children are non-Hispanic white. We are grateful to Sean Reardon and Demetra Kalogrides for also supplying these data.

32. The increase at the 95th percentile was from $153,000 to $223,000. Incomes for the richest families—those in the top .1% of the income distribution—averaged 2–3 times higher in the 2000s relative to their 1970 levels, but showed considerable volatility across the boom and bust year; see http://g-mond.parisschoolofeconomics.eu/topincomes/.

33. In 2011, more than 16 million children lived in households with income below the poverty line. Since economic conditions in 2010 were worse than conditions in 1970, it is useful to note that the child poverty rate for peak economic year 2007 was 18.0%, which is 2.9 percentage points higher than in 1970. Poverty data are taken from http://www.census.gov/hhes/www/poverty/data/historical/people.html.

34. Figure 2.5 is from Michael Hout and Alexander Janus, "Educational Mobility in the United States Since the 1930s," in *Whither Opportunity?*, eds. Duncan and Murnane (2011), 165–186. The analysis is based on data from the General Social Surveys and is drawn from reports of own and parent education for individuals between ages 27 and 64. We choose age 25 to index calendar years. The chapter provides more details about trends in

intergenerational mobility in educational attainments in the U.S. Trends for the relative educational attainments of females and their mothers are similar. For upward mobility, they begin and peak at similar levels and times but decline more slowly than the male trends. For downward mobility, like the male trend depicted in figure 2.5, they rise over the whole period, although more slowly than the male trend beginning around 1970.

35. See *Pursuing the American Dream: Economic Mobility Across Generations*, Washington, D.C.: Pew Charitable Trusts (2012).The Pew Charitable Trusts provides recent evidence on the degree of intergenerational mobility in the United States. It finds that some 84% of grown children have higher incomes than their parents did at a similar age—an impressively high figure. But at the same time, only 50% of grown children have as much wealth as their parents. And for grown sons and their fathers, only 59% of sons out-earned their fathers at the same age. We lack comparable data from earlier generations to determine whether these indicators of intergenerational mobility are smaller now than before. Gary Solon and Chul-In Lee, in "Trends in Intergenerational Income Mobility," *Review of Economics and Statistics* 91 (2009): 766–772, find no evidence of trends in family income mobility for children born between 1952 and 1975 but are unable to observe later cohorts when they are in the middle of their careers.

36. Markus Jantti et al., in "American Exceptionalism in a New Light: A Comparison of Intergenerational Earnings Mobility in the Nordic Countries, the United Kingdom and the United States" (working paper no. 1938, IZA Discussion Papers, Aarhus, Denmark, 2006), calculate a number of measures of earning mobility across countries. Suppose we examine the fraction of sons with low-earning fathers (i.e., fathers whose earnings placed them among the bottom one-fifth of all fathers) who were not low earners themselves (i.e., sons whose earnings placed them among the top four-fifths of all sons). This fraction for the United States (58%) is more than 10 points lower than the comparable figures for the Scandinavian countries and, perhaps surprisingly, the United Kingdom. They calculate a number of measures of earning mobility across countries and all of them agree on the fact that intergenerational earnings mobility appears to be lower in the United States than in the other countries included in their study.

Chapter 3

1. These data are drawn from the Early Childhood Longitudinal Study—Kindergarten Cohort, which tracked children who entered school in the 1998–1999 school year. Figure 3.1 compares children in the highest and lowest quintiles of the income distribution. We appreciate the research assistance of Emily Penner in providing these data. Procedures parallel those described in Greg J. Duncan and Katherine Magnuson, "The Nature and Impact of Early Achievement Skills, Attention Skills, and Behavior Problems," in *Whither Opportunity? Rising Inequality, Schools, and Children's Life Chances*, eds. Greg J. Duncan and Richard J. Murnane (New York: Russell Sage Foundation and the Spencer Foundation, 2011), 47–69, Appendix tables 3.A5 and 3.A6. The Duncan and Magnuson chapter also describes the school engagement, antisocial behavior, and mental health problems measures featured in figure 3.1.

2. Respective gaps in mathematics achievement were 1.15 standard deviations (115 SAT-type points) in kindergarten and the same size in fifth grade.

3. See table 1, p. 14 of Steven J. Ingels, Thomas R. Curtin, Philip Kaufman, Martha N. Alt, and Xianglei Chen, *Coming of Age in the 1990s: The Eighth-Grade Class of 1988 12 Years Later* (Washington, D.C.: U.S. Department of Education, National Center for Education

Statistics,2002), http://nces.ed.gov/pubs2002/2002321.pdf. The report describes the educational outcomes of participants in the National Education Longitudinal Study of 1988. In calculating these high school graduation rates, GED recipients are not treated as high school graduates.

4. Gary Becker, *Human Capital* (New York: National Bureau of Economic Research, 2007), and Robert Haveman and Barbara Wolfe, "The determinants of children's attainments: A review of methods and findings," *Journal of Economic Literature* 33, no. 4 (1995):1829–1878.

5. Vonnie McLoyd, "The impact of economic hardship on black families and children: Psychological distress, parenting, and socioemotional development," *Child Development*, 61, no. 2 (1990): 311–346.

6. Elizabeth Votruba-Drzal, in "Income Changes and Cognitive Stimulation in Young Children's Home Learning Environments," *Journal of Marriage and Family*, 65, no. 2 (2003): 341–355, shows that increases in family income are associated with increases in the level of cognitive stimulation provided by parents to children making the transition into formal schooling.

7. Annette Lareau, *Unequal Childhoods: Class, Race, and Family Life*, 2nd ed. with an Update a Decade Later (Berkeley: University of California Press, 2011).

8. Ibid., 139.

9. Ibid., 139.

10. Gary Evans, in "The environment of childhood poverty, *American Psychologist* 59 (2004): 77–92, provides a review of this evidence, much of which is drawn from correlational studies. See also Gary Evans, P. Kim, A. Ting, H. Tesher, and D. Shannis, "Cumulative risk, maternal responsiveness, and allostatic load among young adolescents," *Developmental Psychology* 43 no. 2 (2007): 341–351, for a study of economic disadvantage and children's stress systems.

11. Data from the 2005–2006 Consumer Expenditure Survey are compiled in Neeraj Kaushal, Katherine Magnuson, and Jane Waldfogel, "How is Family Income Related to Investments in Children's Learning?" in *Whither Opportunity?*, eds. Duncan and Murnane (2011), 187–206. They define "high-income" families to be the richest 20%, while "low-income" comprise the poorest 20%.

12. These data are expressed in 2012 dollars. As defined by Kaushal, Magnuson, and Waldfogel (2011), enrichment expenditures include extracurricular activities (lessons or participation in organized activities such as athletics and Boy Scouts, which do not provide an explicitly academic content); home learning materials (books, computers); and school-related investments (preschool, tutors, and private school attendance). We are very grateful to Sabino Kornrich of the Center for the Advanced Studies in the Social Sciences at the Juan March Institute in Madrid for providing the time-series calculations. See also Sabino Kornrich and Frank Furstenberg, "Investing in Children: Changes in Parental Spending on Children, 1972–2007," *Demography* 50, no. 1 (2013): 1–23. These expenditure data differ from the income data presented in figure 2.4 in two noteworthy ways. First, they are family- rather than child-based. In the case of family income the family-based gap did not grow as rapidly as the child-based gap. Second, the expenditure data show average expenditures for all families in the bottom and top 20% of families. The income data presented in figure 2.4 show 20th, 80th and 95th percentiles of the income distribution.

13. Kaushal et al. (2011).

14. Key references regarding parenting stress, all of which rely on correlational evidence, include McLoyd (1990); P. Lindsay Chase-Lansdale and Laura Pittman, "Welfare reform

and parenting: Reasonable expectations," *Future of Children* 12 (2002): 167–185; and Vonnie McLoyd, T. E. Jayaratne, R. Ceballo, and J. Borquez, "Unemployment and work interruption among African American single mothers: Effects on parenting and adolescent socioemotional functioning," *Child Development* 65 (1994): 562–589.

15. Diana Baumrind, "Current patterns of parental authority," *Developmental Psychology* 4, no. 1, part 2 (1971): 1–103; W. Jean Yeung, Miriam R. Linver, and Jeanne Brooks-Gunn, "How Money Matters for Young Children's Development: Parental Investment and Family Processes," *Child Development* 73, no. 6 (Nov.–Dec. 2002): 1861–1879.

16. These connections are described in C. Zahn-Waxler, S. Duggal, and R. Gruber, "Parental Psychopathology," in *Handbook of Parenting*, 2nd ed., ed. M. H. Bornstein (Mahwah, NJ: Lawrence Erlbaum, 2002), 4:95–328.

17. William Evans and Craig Garthwaite, "Giving mom a break: The impact of higher EITC payments on maternal health" (NBER Working Paper No. 16296, Cambridge, MA: National Bureau of Economic Research, 2010). This study took advantage of the fact that the increase in EITC payments was much larger for families with two or more children than just one child. Their analysis of data from the National Health Examination and Nutrition Survey showed that low-SES mothers with two or more children, when compared with mothers with just one child, experienced larger reductions in risky biomarkers and self-reported better mental health. Mental health improvements are also found in Kevin Milligan and Mark Stabile, "Do Child Tax Benefits Affect the Well-being of Children? Evidence from Canadian Child Benefit Expansions," *American Economic Journal: Economic Policy* 3 (2011): 175–205.

18. Rebecca Maynard and Richard J. Murnane, "The effects of a negative income tax on school performance: Results of an experiment," *Journal of Human Resources* 14, no. 4 (1979): 463–476, drew data from the Gary Income Maintenance Experiment, which was conducted 40 years ago to assess the effects of Richard Nixon's Family Assistance Plan proposal. Rebecca Maynard, in "The effects of the Rural Income Maintenance Experiment on the school performance of children," *American Economic Review* 67, no. 1 (1977): 370–375, analyzes data from two rural sites in the same experiment.

19. Pamela Morris et al., *How Welfare and Work Policies Affect Children: A Synthesis of Research* (New York: MDRC, 2001).

20. The estimate comes from Greg Duncan, Pamela Morris, and Chris Rodrigues, "Does money matter? Estimating impacts of family income on young children's achievement with data from random-assignment experiments," *Developmental Psychology* 47, no. 5 (2011): 1263–1279. Two additional studies with strong methods that also find links between increased income and high child achievement are Gordon B. Dahl and Lance Lochner, "The Impact of Family Income on Child Achievement: Evidence from the Earned Income Tax Credit," *American Economic Review* 102 (2012): 1927–1956, and Milligan and Stabile, "Do Child Tax Benefits Affect the Well-being of Children?" (see note 17).

21. Based on the much larger literature, the magnitude of income effects is a matter of considerable debate. See, for example, Susan Mayer, *What Money Can't Buy* (Cambridge, MA: Harvard University Press, 1997), David Blau, "The Effect of Income on Child Development," *Review of Economics and Statistics* 81, no. 2 (1999): 261–276 and Greg J. Duncan et al., "Early-Childhood Poverty and Adult Attainment, Behavior, and Health," *Child Development* 81 (2010): 306–325. Another issue in this literature is whether providing income supplements to families based on their behavior is more effective than simple unconditional transfers. The income supplements from the Earned Income Tax Credit

and in the welfare-to-work experiments were conditioned on demonstrated work effort. In the Gary Income Maintenance experiment, nothing was required of the recipients, although the amount of the income supplement declined at higher levels of family income from other sources. M. Lagarde, A. Haines, and N. Palmer, in "Conditional Cash Transfers for Improving Uptake of Health Interventions in Low- and Middle-Income Countries: A Systematic Review," *JAMA* 298, no.16 (2007):1900–1910, summarize mostly positive results from the more general literature on conditional cash transfers, most of which is based on programs in developing countries. One such program in the United States did not produce strong positive results; see James Riccio, Nadine Dechausay, David Greenberg, Cynthia Miller, Zawadi Rucks, and Nandita Verma, *Toward Reduced Poverty Across Generations: Early Findings from New York City's Conditional Cash Transfer Program* (New York: MDRC, 2010).

22. A general review of the literature on single-parent families is provided in Sara McLanahan and Christine Percheski, "Family structure and the reproduction of inequalities," *Annual Review of Sociology* 34 (2008): 257–276. Among the results summarized in this review article are that the increase in single-parent families accounts for between 11% and 62% of increase in family income inequality, depending on the study and the time period, and that the weight of the evidence supports the idea that single motherhood lowers children's future life chances by reducing parental resources (income and mental health) and undermining the quality of parenting. A more recent study documenting gender differences is Marianne Bertrand and Jessica Pan, "The Trouble with Boys: Social Influences and the Gender Gap in Disruptive Behavior," *American Economic Journal. Applied Economics* 5, no. 1 (Jan. 2013): 1–35.

23. Bertrand and Pan, "The Trouble with Boys" (see note 22).

24. See, for example, K. Magnuson, "Maternal education and children's academic achievement during middle childhood," *Developmental Psychology* 43, no. 6 (2007): 1497–1512, doi: http://dx.doi.org/10.1037/0012-1649.43.6.1497.

25. A summary of their study and its results are given in Betty Hart and Todd Risley, *Meaningful Differences in the Everyday Experience of Young American Children* (Baltimore, MD: Brookes Publishing Company, 1998).

26. For example, Hart and Risley found that affirmations were six times more likely than prohibitions for professional parents, whereas for welfare families prohibitions were twice as likely as affirmations.

27. Duncan et al. (2011), who draw data from the ECLS-K.

28. Mayer (1997) provides many details behind this argument.

29. G. S. Pettit, P. E. Davis-Kean, and K. Magnuson, "Educational attainment in developmental perspective: Longitudinal analyses of continuity, change, and process," *Merrill-Palmer Quarterly* 55 (2009): 217–223.

30. Lareau, *Unequal Childhoods*, 35, 66–67.

Chapter 4

1. Tracy Kidder, *Among Schoolchildren* (Boston: Houghton Mifflin, 1989).

2. Ibid., 52.

3. Claudia D. Goldin and Lawrence F. Katz, *The Race Between Education and Technology* (Cambridge, MA: Belknap Press of Harvard University Press, 2008).

4. As described in chapter 2, this evidence comes from combining NAEP data on trends in average math achievement between 1978 and 2009 with trends in the achievement scores of

children at the 90th and 10th percentiles of the income distribution, from Sean F. Reardon, "The Widening Academic Achievement Gap Between the Rich and the Poor: New Evidence and Possible Explanations," in *Whither Opportunity? Rising Inequality, Schools, and Children's Life Chances*, eds. Greg J. Duncan and Richard J. Murnane (New York: Russell Sage Foundation and the Spencer Foundation, 2011). Children at the 10th income percentile gained 40 points in mathematics achievement on an SAT-type scale. Children at the 90th income percentile gained 75 points—nearly twice as much.

5. National Commission on Excellence in Education, *A Nation at Risk: The Imperative for Educational Reform* (Washington, D.C.: U.S. Department of Education, 1983), 5.

6. Center on Education Policy, *State High School Tests: Exit Exams and Other Assessments* (Washington, D.C.: CEP, 2010).

7. This item comes from Kidder, *Among Schoolchildren*, 199.

8. Taken from the set of released items from the 2011 Massachusetts Comprehensive Assessment System grade 6 mathematics examination, available at http://www.doe.mass.edu/mcas/2011/release/.

9. For example, as part of its educational reform initiative, Massachusetts invested heavily in improving the quality of education provided in the state's public schools. This produced improvements in mathematics and reading skills, as measured by scores on National Assessment of Educational Progress examinations, for students from a wide range of family backgrounds. For evidence that income-based gaps in student outcomes in Massachusetts have declined in recent years, see John P. Papay, Richard J. Murnane, and John B. Willett, *Income-Based Inequality in Educational Outcomes: Learning from State Longitudinal Data Systems* (Washington, D.C.: paper prepared for the Society for Research on Educational Effectiveness Annual Meeting, 2013).

10. For a discussion of the evidence that increases in high school graduation requirements have had a negative impact on high school graduations for low-income and minority students, see Richard J. Murnane, "U.S High School Graduation Rates: Patterns and Explanations," *Journal of Economic Literature* 51, no. 2 (June 2013): 370–422. Although not without exceptions, the evidence indicates generally that increased graduation requirements have reduced high school graduation rates among low-achieving students (including those with learning disabilities), students of color, and urban low-income students. For example, Brian A. Jacob, in "Getting Tough? The Impact of High School Graduation Exams," *Educational Evaluation and Policy Analysis* 23, no. 2 (Summer 2001): 99–121, and John H. Bishop et al., in "The Role of End-of-Course Exams and Minimal Competency Exams in Standards-Based Reforms," *Brookings Papers in Education Policy 2001*, ed. Diane Ravitch (Washington, D.C.: Brookings, 2001), find that increased requirements reduced high school graduation rates of low-achieving students by 6% to 7%. Thomas S. Dee and Brian A. Jacob, in "Do High School Exit Exams Influence Educational Attainment or Labor Market Performance?" *Standards-Based Reform and Children in Poverty: Lessons for "No Child Left Behind,"* ed. Adam Gamoran (Washington, D.C.: Brookings Institution Press, 2007), also report negative, albeit considerably smaller, impacts of minimum competency tests on the high school graduation rates of particular disadvantaged groups. The pattern is somewhat stronger, although again with some exceptions, on the impacts of more difficult standards-based exit examinations that states have adopted during the last two decades. Sean Reardon and Michal Kurlaender, in *Effects of the California High School Exit Exam on Student Persistence, Achievement, and Graduation* (Stanford, CA: PACE Policy Brief, 2009), and Sean F. Reardon et al., in "Effects of the California High School Exit Exam Requirement on

Student Persistence, Achievement, and Graduation" (working paper, Stanford University, 2010), use data on three cohorts of students from four large California school districts to examine these impacts and find that the introduction of exit examinations reduced high school graduation rates by approximately 4 percentage points, with effects concentrated among low-achieving students, minority students, and English language learners. John R. Warren, Krista N. Jenkins, and Rachael Kulick, in "High School Exit Examinations and State-Level Completion and GED Rates, 1975–2002," *Educational Evaluation and Policy Analysis* 28 (2006): 131–152, and Dee and Jacob, "Do High School Exit Exams," report that exit exam requirements reduced high school graduation rates by about 2 percentage points, with larger effects in states with more difficult examinations, and with effects concentrated among black students and among students in districts with large percentages of students of color. Steven W. Hemelt and Dave E. Marcott, in "High School Exit Exams and Dropout in an Era of Increased Accountability," *Journal of Policy Analysis and Management* 32, no. 2 (Spring 2013): 323–349, report results similar to those of Dee and Jacob.

11. Catherine E. Snow and Connie Juel, "Teaching Children to Read: What Do We Know about How to Do It?" in *The Science of Reading: A Handbook*, eds. Margaret J. Snowling and Charles Hulme (Oxford, UK: Blackwell, 2005), 501–520. Reading textbooks are often called basal readers in the academic literature on reading instruction.

12. For a description of balanced literacy, see http://www.fcps.edu/CrossfieldES/Parent%20 Resources/Balanced_Literacy.pdf.

13. See Sean F. Reardon and Kendra Bischoff, "Income Inequality and Income Segregation," *American Journal of Sociology* 116, no. 4 (2011): 1092–1153, table C1: 1147. They develop an isolation index that varies from 0 (complete mixing of families from different incomes classes) to 1 (complete residential segregation). The index increased from .18 to .22 for high-income families (90th percentile of income distribution) and from .12 to .18 for low-income families (10th percentile). These trends toward increased residential segregation by income are also found in Paul A. Jargowsky, *Poverty and Place: Ghettos, Barrios, and the American City* (New York: Russell Sage Foundation, 1997) and Tara Watson, "Inequality and the Measurement of Residential Segregation by Income in American Neighborhoods," *Review of Income and Wealth* 55, no. 3 (Sept. 2009): 820–844. All three studies point to the 1980s as the time in which much of this increase occurred.

14. Edward Glaeser and Jacob Vigdor, *The End of the Segregated Century: Racial Separation in America's Neighborhoods, 1890–2010* (Manhattan Institute for Policy Research: Civil Report Number 66, 2012), http://www.manhattan-institute.org/pdf/cr_66.pdf.

15. These data are from Joseph G. Altonji and Richard Mansfield, "The Role of Family, School and Community Characteristics in Inequality in Education and Labor Market Outcomes," in *Whither Opportunity?*, eds. Duncan and Murnane (2011).This study scales income in natural logarithmic units. As with residential segregation, the jump in the school-based income gap appears to have taken place largely in the 1980s.

16. In this context, we define high-poverty schools as those in which more than half of the students are eligible for a free or reduced-price lunch. We define high-income schools as those in which less than 5% of the students are eligible for a free or reduced-price lunch. The data are from Greg J. Duncan and Katherine Magnuson, "The Nature and Impact of Early Achievement Skills, Attention Skills, and Behavior Problems," in *Whither Opportunity?*, eds. Duncan and Murnane (2011), 47–70.

17. Kidder, *Among Schoolchildren*, 3–16. All of the students' names in the Kidder book are pseudonyms.

18. Ibid., 87–88.
19. Ibid., 115–116
20. Mimi Engel, "Problematic Preferences? A Mixed Method Examination of Principals' Preferences When Hiring Teachers," *Educational Administration Quarterly* 49, no. 1 (Feb. 2013): 52–91.
21. Ibid, 69.
22. 223.
23. The idea behind this approach is that while children may not be randomly assigned to particular classrooms, the fraction of students exposed to domestic violence does vary fairly randomly from one school year to the next; see Scott E. Carrell and Mark L. Hoekstra, "Externalities in the Classroom: How Children Exposed to Domestic Violence Affect Everyone's Kids," *American Economic Journal: Applied Economics* 2, no. 1 (Jan. 2010): 211–228.
24. Anna Aizer, in "Peer Effects and Human Capital Accumulation: The Externalities of ADD" (working paper no. 13354, National Bureau of Economic Research, Cambridge, MA, 2008), documents the achievement gains surrounding the diagnoses of attention disorders.
25. Peter Rossi, *Why Families Move* (Glencoe, IL: Free Press, 1955). Census Bureau data show that, between 2009 and 2010, 17.0% of householders with incomes under $20,000 moved as compared with 6.5% of householders with incomes above $100,000. See http://www.census.gov/hhes/migration/data/cps/cps2010.html.
26. Stephen W. Raudenbush, Marshall Jean, and Emily Art, "Year-by-Year and Cumulative Impacts of Attending a High-Mobility Elementary School on Children's Mathematics Achievement in Chicago, 1995–2005," in *Whither Opportunity?*, eds. Duncan and Murnane (2011), 359–376.
27. These data come from http://www.urban.org/publications/900884.html.
28. Amy Ellen Schwartz and Leanna Stiefel, "Immigrants and Inequality in Public Schools," in *Whither Opportunity?*, eds. Duncan and Murnane (2011), 419–441.
29. Raj Chetty, John N. Friedman, and Jonah H. Rockoff, *The Long-Term Impacts of Teachers: Teacher Value-Added and Student Outcomes in Adulthood* (Cambridge, MA: working paper no. 17699, National Bureau of Economic Research, 2011); Terry Tivnan and Lowry Hemphill, "Comparing Four Literacy Reform Models in High Poverty Schools: Patterns of First-Grade Achievement," *Elementary School Journal* 105, no. 5 (2005): 419–441.
30. Jonah E. Rockoff, "The Impact of Individual Teachers of Student Achievement: Evidence from Panel Data," *American Economic Review, Papers and Proceedings* 94, no. 2 (2004): 247–252.
31. C. Kirabo Jackson and Elias Bruegmann, "Teaching Students and Teaching Each Other: The Importance of Peer Learning for Teachers," *American Economic Journal: Applied Economics* 1, no. 4 (Oct. 2009): 85–108.
32. Geoffrey D. Borman and N. Maritza Dowling, "Teacher Attrition and Retention: A Meta-Analytic and Narrative Review of the Research," *Review of Educational Research* 78, no. 3 (Sept. 2008): 367–409; Eric A. Hanushek, John F. Kain, and Steven G. Rivkin, "Why Public Schools Lose Teachers," *Journal of Human Resources* 39, no. 2 (2004): 326–354.
33. Tim R. Sass et al., *Value Added of Teachers in High-Poverty Schools and Lower Poverty Schools* (Washington, D.C.: CALDER working paper no. 52, Urban Institute, 2010).
34. Sarah C. Fuller and Helen F. Ladd, "School Based Accountability and the Distribution of Teacher Quality among Grades in Elementary Schools" (working paper no. 75, CALDER, Washington, DC, 2012).

35. Donald Boyd et al., "The Effect of School Neighborhoods on Teachers' Career Decisions," in *Whither Opportunity?*, eds. Duncan and Murnane (2011), 377–396.
36. Donald Boyd et al., "The Draw of Home: How Teachers' Preferences for Proximity Disadvantage Urban Schools," *Journal of Policy Analysis and Management* 24, no. 1 (2005): 113–132.
37. To illustrate the extent to which children from low-income families have less access to effective teachers than children from middle-class families, we draw on a recent study conducted for the Institute of Education Sciences. The authors ranked middle-school mathematics teachers in a large public school district (call it District A) by their effectiveness in enhancing their students' scores on standardized mathematics tests. They classified the 20% of teachers with the most success as "highest performing." They then divided the district's middle schools into five groups (quintiles) ranked by the poverty rate among students. Finally, they calculated the percentage of "highest performing" teachers who taught in middle schools in each quintile. In this district, only 6% of the best mathematics teachers taught in the schools serving the highest concentration of low-income students, while 62% of them taught in schools with the lowest percentage of low-income students. In other districts, the unequal distribution of effective teachers was not as stark as it was in District A. However, the overall pattern was that middle-school students in high-poverty schools in most districts included in the study have less access to the best teachers than do middle school students in schools serving primarily non-poor children. For more details, see National Center for Education Evaluation and Regional Assistance, *Do Low-Income Students Have Equal Access to the Highest-Performing Teachers?* (Washington, D.C.: Institute of Education Sciences, U.S. Department of Education, 2011).
38. Susan M. Johnson, Matthew A. Kraft, and John P. Papay, "How Context Matters in High-Need Schools: The Effects of Teachers' Working Conditions on Their Professional Satisfaction and Their Students' Achievement," *Teachers College Record* 114, no. 10 (2012).
39. David K. Cohen and Susan L. Moffitt, *The Ordeal of Equality: Did Federal Regulation Fix the Schools?* (Cambridge, MA: Harvard University Press, 2009). The authors use the term "educational infrastructure" in place of our term "school supports." They explain the meaning and importance of this term in considerable detail. W. Norton Grubb, in *The Money Myth: Schools, Resources, Outcomes, and Equity* (New York: Russell Sage Foundation, 2009), also provides an informative discussion of the importance of school supports.
40. The dysfunctional responses include focusing undue attention on the subset of students whose scores are close to meeting benchmarks for adequate performance and changing students' scores on examinations used in accountability systems. For evidence of the first type of response, see Derek Neal and Diane Whitmore Schanzenbach, "Left Behind by Design: Proficiency Counts and Test-Based Accountability," *Review of Economics and Statistics* 92, no. 2 (May 2010): 263–283. For evidence on the second type of response, see Brian A. Jacob and Steven D. Levitt, "Rotten Apples: An Investigation of the Prevalence and Predictors of Teacher Cheating," *Quarterly Journal of Economics* 118, no. 3 (Aug. 2003): 843–877.

Chapter 5

1. Eric I. Knudsen et al., "Economic, Neurobiological, and Behavioral Perspectives on Building America's Future Workforce," *Proceedings of the National Academy of Sciences of the United States of America* 103 (2006): 10155–62; Jack Shonkoff and Deborah Phillips, eds., *From Neurons to Neighborhoods: The Science of Early Childhood Development* (Washington, D.C.: National Academy Press, 2000).

2. Charles Nelson and Margaret Sheridan, "Lessons from Neuroscience Research for Understanding Causal Links Between Family and Neighborhood Characteristics and Educational Outcomes," in *Whither Opportunity? Rising Inequality, Schools, and Children's Life Chances*, eds. Greg J. Duncan and Richard J. Murnane (New York: Russell Sage Foundation and the Spencer Foundation, 2011), 27–46.

3. Flavio Cunha and James J. Heckman, "The Technology of Skill Formation," *American Economic Review* 97, no. 2 (2007): 31–47.

4. Greg Duncan et al., "School Readiness and Later Achievement," *Developmental Psychology* 43, no. 8 (2007): 1428–1446.

5. National Scientific Council on the Developing Child, "Building the Brain's 'Air Traffic Control' System: How Early Experiences Shape the Development of Executive Function" (working paper no. 11, Center on the Developing Child, Harvard University, Cambridge, MA, 2012), http://developingchild.harvard.edu/index.php/resources/reports_and_working_papers/working_papers/wp11/.

6. See Lawrence J. Schweinhart et al., *Lifetime Effects: The High/Scope Perry Preschool Study Through Age 40* (Ypsilanti, MI: High/Scope Press, 2005); James Heckman et al., "The Rate of Return to the High/Scope Perry Preschool Program" (working paper no. 15471, National Bureau of Economic Research, Cambridge, MA, 2009); F. Ramey Campbell et al., "Early Childhood Education: Young Adult Outcomes from the Abecedarian Project," *Applied Developmental Science* 6, no. 1 (2002): 42–57.

7. Very few child-care centers would have existed in the neighborhoods of Perry and Abecedarian children. In contrast, the recent National Head Start Impact Study found that nearly 50% of the four-year-old children who lost the lottery to enter their first-choice Head Start center attended some other kind of center-based child care. See Mike Puma, Stephen Bell, Ronna Cook, Camilla Heid, Pam Broene, Frank Jenkins, Andrew Mashburn, and Jason Downer, *Third Grade Follow-up to the Head Start Impact Study Final Report*, OPRE Report # 2012-45 (Washington, D.C.: Office of Planning, Research and Evaluation, Administration for Children and Families, U.S. Department of Health and Human Services, 2012).

8. This and the maternal schooling point made below are documented in Greg J. Duncan and Katherine Magnuson, "Investing in Preschool Programs," *Journal of Economic Perspectives* 27, no. 2 (Spring 2013): 109–132.

9. Jens Ludwig and Deborah Phillips, "The Benefits and Costs of Head Start," *Social Policy Report* 21 (2007): 3–20.

10. The per-child cost estimate comes from Jens Ludwig and Deborah A. Phillips, "Long-Term Effects of Head Start on Low-Income Children," *Annals of the New York Academy of Science* 1136 (2008).

11. In November 2011 President Obama announced new rules aimed at increasing the accountability of Head Start programs. See Maggie Severns, "Long-Term Effects of Head Start on Low-Income Children," *Salon*, Nov. 8, 2011, http://www.salon.com/topic/head_start/.

12. David Deming, in "Early Childhood Intervention and Life-Cycle Skill Development: Evidence from Head Start," *American Economic Journal: Applied Economics* 1, no. 3 (July 2009): 111–134, provides a recent look at these kinds of sibling differences. Another historical study finding long-term benefits is Jens Ludwig and Douglas L. Miller, "Does Head Start Improve Children's Life Chances? Evidence from a Regression Discontinuity Design," *Quarterly Journal of Economics* 122, no. 1 (Feb. 2007): 159–208.

13. Puma et al., *Third Grade Follow-up*.

14. For an interesting discussion of alternative explanations of the findings from recent evaluations of Head Start, see Chloe Gibbs, Jens Ludwig, and Douglas L. Miller, *Does Head Start Do Any Lasting Good?* (Cambridge, MA: NBER working paper 17452, 2011).

15. Deborah A. Phillips, William T. Gormley, and A. E. Lowenstein, "Inside the Pre-Kindergarten Door: Classroom Climate and Instructional Time Allocation in Tulsa's Pre-K Program," *Early Childhood Research Quarterly* (in press).

16. The National Institute for Early Education Research at Rutgers University tracks the number and quality of these programs; see http://nieer.org/.

17. Vivian C. Wong, "An Effectiveness-Based Evaluation of Five State Pre-Kindergarten Programs," *Journal of Policy Analysis and Management* 27, no. 1 (Jan. 2008): 122–154.

18. William T. Gormley Jr., Deborah Phillips, and Ted Gayer, in "Preschool Programs Can Boost School Readiness," *Science* 320, no. 5884 (2008): 1723–1724, present the Tulsa results. In contrast to the lottery-based evaluations of the recent national evaluation of Head Start studies, these preK program evaluations rely on what is called a regression discontinuity design. To be eligible for most preK programs, a child must turn four years of age as of some date—in Boston's case, September 1. In September of any given year, it is possible to measure the skills and knowledge of five-year-old children whose parents had enrolled them in the preK program in the previous school year. But at the same time one can measure those same skills and knowledge of children who had missed the age cutoff for last year's preK program. Focusing the analysis on the children with birthdays closest to the birthday cutoff point provides two very similar groups of children—one of which has just completed a year of preK and the other who were forced to opt for alternative-care arrangements. As Gibbs, Ludwig, and Miller, in *Does Head Start Do Any Lasting Good?* (2011), explain, a limitation of the design of the Gormley, Phillips, and Gayer (2008) and Weiland and Yoshikawa (2013) studies is that it is not possible to examine the long-term effects of the preK programs. The reason is that the comparison group participates in the preK program the year after the treatment group does.

19. National data on these differences are documented in chapter 3.

20. We calculated the 9 percentage point figure using data available on the Boston Public Schools website.

21. Tracy Jan, "Boston Preschools Falling Far Short of Goals, Study Says," *Boston Globe*, sec. A, April 7, 2007.

22. Personal interview with Jason Sachs on November 9, 2011.

23. The description of the Boston preK program draws heavily on Christina Weiland and Hirokazu Yoshikawa, "Impacts of a Prekindergarten Program on Children's Mathematics, Language, Literacy, Executive Function, and Emotional Skills," *Child Development* (March 2013), doi:10.1111/cdev.12099.

24. Nancy L. Marshall and Joanne Roberts, *Boston Public Schools Early Childhood Quality Study* (Wellesley, MA: Wellesley Centers for Women, 2010).

25. 43% of PreK participants scored at the proficient or advanced level on the grade 3 MCAS ELA examination compared to 34% of nonparticipants. The black-white gap in the percentage of 3rd graders who scored at the proficient or advanced level on the MCAS ELA examination was 14.3 percentage points compared to 22.9 percentage points among nonparticipants. The source of this information is a report Jason Sachs presented to the BPS School Committee in 2011. One limitation of this evidence is that the higher 3rd-grade achievement of children who participated in the BPS preK program could stem,

in part, from differences between the family environments of participants and non-participants.

26. Weiland and Yoshikawa, in "Impacts of a Prekindergarten Program (2013), use the regression discontinuity design for their impact assessment. This method is described in an earlier endnote in this chapter. For a more detailed exposition of the method, see Richard J. Murnane and John B. Willett, *Methods Matter: Improving Causal Inference in Educational and Social Science Research* (New York: Oxford University Press, 2011).

27. The differences amounted to between one-half to three-quarters of a standard deviation higher, which translates into 50 to 75 points on a test that employs an SAT-type scoring scale.

28. One of the simplest tests for the impulse control element of executive functioning is the pencil tap test. In it, the tester gives a pencil to the child and instructs him or her to tap the pencil once if the tester taps twice, and to tap the pencil twice if the tester taps once. This requires the child to suppress the impulse to imitate what the tester does—a surprisingly difficult task for some four- and five-year-olds.

29. Duncan and Magnuson, "Investing in Preschool Programs" (2013).

30. This is on top of the Head Start program, which enrolled an additional 11% of four-year-olds in 2011. See W. Steven Barnett et al., *The State of Preschool 2011: State Preschool Yearbook* (New Brunswick, NJ: National Institute for Early Education Research, 2011).

31. Ibid.

32. According to Weiland and Hirokazu Yoshikawa (2013), the educational requirements and pay scales for Boston's preK teachers were identical to those of other public school teachers. In particular, the teachers must have at least a bachelor's degree and obtain a master's degree within five years. In the 2008–2009 academic year, 78% of program teachers held masters degrees and 75% had at least five years of teaching experience. According to W. Steven Barnett et al. (2011), 29 out of 39 states required a BA for teachers in state-funded prekindergarten programs. Boston's $12,000 per-student cost is more than twice as high as the $4,847 per-pupil cost reported in W. Steven Barnett et al. (2011). Impacts from five state preK program are given in Wong et al. (2008); see also Gormley, Phillips, and Gayer (2008).

Chapter 6

1. NKO teachers use the term "mini-lesson" to refer to the direct instruction on a particular topic (like Bossy Rs) that each teacher provides to her whole class at the beginning of each day's literacy block. Some teachers, like Erica Emmendorfer, start the mini-lesson during meeting time, which precedes the two-hour literacy block. The mini-lesson is a component of the balanced literacy approach that the school has embraced since it opened its doors in 1998.

2. Reading experts debate the relative merits of requiring all children to read the same, relatively demanding texts while providing the appropriate amount of scaffolding, and allowing students to build reading skills by choosing "just right" texts. For example, see Kathleen Porter-Magee's blog, "Common Core Opens the Second Front in the Reading Wars," August 15, 2012, available at http://shankerblog.org/?p=6506 .The NKO approach attempts to do both, with time devoted to helping students understand a relatively demanding text such as *The Trumpet of the Swan*, while also encouraging children's interest in reading by letting them choose books to read during daily reading time.

3. The University of Chicago Charter School does not use the term "network." Instead it refers to itself as a school with four campuses, each of which has its own principal. We adopt

"network" because it is commonly used to describe the group of schools that are affiliated with a charter management organization.

4. These achievement differences are substantial, especially when compared with the results of other policy initiatives aimed at increasing the achievement of children from low-income families. For example, reducing class size in grades K–3 from 22–25 students to 13–17 students, an extremely expensive, well-known policy experiment conducted in Tennessee in the mid-1980s, increased students' reading skills by approximately 0.22 standard deviations. See Alan B. Krueger, "Experimental Estimates of Education Production Functions," *Quarterly Journal of Economics* 114, no. 2 (May 1999): 497–532.

5. Will Dobbie and Roland G. Fryer, "Getting Beneath the Veil of Effective Schools: Evidence from New York City," *American Economic Journal. Applied Economics* (forthcoming).

6. For more on NKO's successful strategy, see the insightful book by Elizabeth McGhee Hassrick, Stephen W. Raudenbush, and Lisa Rosen, *The Ambitious Elementary School: Its Conception, Design and Contribution to Educational Equity* (Chicago: University of Chicago Press, forthcoming).

7. For an insightful description of teaching in the United States, see David K. Cohen, *Teaching and its Predicaments* (Cambridge, MA: Harvard University Press, 2011).

8. For more information on changes in skill demands, see Frank Levy and Richard J. Murnane, *The New Division of Labor: How Computers Are Creating the Next Labor Market* (Princeton, NJ: Princeton University Press, 2004).

9. See John E. Chubb and Terry M. Moe, *Politics, Markets, and America's Schools* (Washington, D.C.: Brookings, 1990).

10. *Urban School Superintendents: Characteristics, Tenure, and Salary: Seventh Survey and Report* (Council of Great City Schools, Fall 2010).

11. For a rich description of a classic school district bureaucracy, see David Rogers, *110 Livingston Street: Politics and Bureaucracy in the New York City Schools* (New York: Random House, 1968). For more recent evidence, see Charles M. Payne, *So Much Reform, So Little Change: The Persistence of Failure in Urban Schools* (Cambridge, MA: Harvard Education Press, 2008).

12. Atila Abdulkadiroglu et al., "Accountability and Flexibility in Public Schools: Evidence from Boston's Charters and Pilots," *Quarterly Journal of Economics* 126, no. 2 (May 2011): 699–748; Joshua D. Angrist et al., "Inputs and Impacts in Charter Schools: KIPP Lynn," *American Economic Review* 100, no. 2 (May 2010): 239–243; Will Dobbie and Roland G. Fryer Jr., "Are High Quality Schools Enough to Close the Achievement Gap? Evidence from a Social Experiment in Harlem," *American Economic Journal, Applied Economics* (2011): 158–187; Caroline M. Hoxby and Sonali Murarka, "Charter Schools in New York City: Who Enrolls and How They Affect Their Students' Achievement" (working paper no. 14852, National Bureau of Economic Research, Cambridge, MA, 2009). For a discussion of the limitations of existing research on charter schools, see Julian R. Betts and Richard C. Atkinson, "Better Research Needed on the Impact of Charter Schools," *Science* (Jan. 13, 2012). These authors point out that only about 90 oversubscribed charter schools, less than 2% of the total number of charter schools in the U.S., have been included in the studies cited above that find large positive effects.

13. Julian R. Betts and Y. Elizabeth Tang, *The Effects of Charter Schools on Student Achievement: A Meta-Analysis of the Literature* (Bothell, WA: National Charter School Research Project, Center on Reinventing Public Education, 2011). Also, Center for Research on Education Outcomes, *Multiple Choice: Charter School Performance in 16 States* (Palo Alto, CA: CREO, Stanford University, 2009).

14. Steven F. Wilson, "Success at Scale in Charter Schooling" (working paper 2008-02, AEI Future of American Education Project, American Enterprise Institute, Washington, D.C., 2008), 4. This same quotation is used in David K. Cohen and Susan L. Moffitt, *The Ordeal of Equality: Did Federal Regulation Fix the Schools?* (Cambridge, MA: Harvard University Press, 2009), 14.

15. Frederick M. Hess, "'Whaddya Mean You Want to Close My School?' The Politics of Regulatory Accountability in Charter Schooling," *Education and Urban Society* 33, no. 2 (2001): 141–156.

16. For more information about charter management organizations, see Joshua Furgeson et al., *Charter-School Management Organizations: Diverse Strategies and Diverse Student Impacts* (Princeton, NJ: Mathematica Policy Research and Center on Reinventing Public Education, 2012).

17. An exception to the usual pattern is Montgomery County, Maryland, a large district that made considerable progress in improving the education of low-income and minority-group children during the exceptionally long 12-year tenure of Superintendent Jerry Weast. See Stacey M. Childress, Denis P. Doyle, and David A. Thomas, *Leading for Equity: The Pursuit of Excellence in Montgomery County Public Schools* (Cambridge, MA: Harvard Education Press, 2009).

18. Eric A. Hanushek, "The Failure of Input-Based Schooling Policies," *Economic Journal* 113 (2003): F64–F98.

19. This section draws heavily on the arguments and evidence presented in Cohen and Moffitt, *The Ordeal of Equality.*

20. For a description of Success for All and America's Choice, see Brian P. Rowan et al., "School Improvement by Design," in *Handbook of Education Policy Research*, eds. Gary Sykes, Barbara Schneider, and David N. Plank (New York: Routledge, 2009), 637–651.

21. Geoffrey D. Borman, "Final Reading Outcomes of the National Randomized Field Trial of Success For All," *American Educational Research Journal* 44, no. 3 (2007): 701–731; Brian Rowan, "Intervening to Improve the Educational Outcomes of Students in Poverty: Lessons from Recent Work in High-Poverty Schools," in *Whither Opportunity? Rising Inequality, Schools, and Children's Life Chances*, eds. Greg J. Duncan and Richard J. Murnane (New York: Russell Sage Foundation and Spencer Foundation, 2011), 523–538.

22. For an insightful description of Success for All and it accomplishments and limitations, see Donald J. Peurach, *Seeing Complexity in Public Education: Problems, Possibilities, and Success for All* (New York: Oxford University Press, 2011).

23. National Center for Education Evaluation and Regional Assistance, *Do Low-Income Students Have Equal Access to the Highest-Performing Teachers?* (Washington, D.C.: Institute of Education Sciences, U.S. Department of Education, 2011); Susanna Loeb, Demetra Kalogrides, and Tara Beteille, "Effective Schools: Teacher Hiring, Assignment, Development, and Retention," *Education Finance and Policy* 7, no. 3 (2011): 269–304; Charles T. Clotfelter et al., "High-Poverty Schools and the Distribution of Teachers and Principals," *North Carolina Law Review* 85 (2007): 1345–1379.

Chapter 7

1. We use pseudonyms for students and their parents.

2. Evidence on test score gaps between kindergarten and 5th grade is provided by Greg J. Duncan and Katherine Magnuson, "The Nature and Impact of Early Achievement Skills, Attention Skills, and Behavior Problems," in *Whither Opportunity? Rising Inequality,*

Schools, and Children's Life Chances, eds. Greg J. Duncan and Richard J. Murnane (New York: Russell Sage and Spencer Foundations, 2011), 47–70. Evidence on gaps between 8th and 12th grades is provided by George Farkas, "Middle and High School Skills, Behaviors, Attitudes, and Curriculum Enrollment, and their Consequences," in *Whither Opportunity?*, eds. Duncan and Murnane (2011).

3. James J. Heckman and Paul A. LaFontaine, "The American High School Graduation Rate:Trends and Levels," *Review of Economics and Statistics* 92, no. 2 (May 2010): 244–262, table 3, p. 254.

4. NYC Department of Education Progress Report 2011–12 for the Urban Assembly School for Law and Justice, available as a pdf file at http://schools.nyc.gov/Accountability/tools/report/FindAProgressReport/default.htm.

5. For information on career academies, see James J. Kemple, *Career Academies: Long-Term Impacts on Labor Market Outcomes, Educational Attainment, and Transitions to Adulthood* (New York: MDRC, 2008). For information on early-college high schools, see Julie A. Edmunds et al., "Expanding the Start of the College Pipeline: Ninth-Grade Findings from an Experimental Study of the Impact of the Early College High School Model," *Journal of Research on Educational Effectiveness* 5, no. 2 (2012), and Julie A. Edmunds et al., "Keeping Students in School: Impact of a High School Reform Model on Students' Enrollment and Progression in School" (paper presented at the Annual Meetings of the American Educational Research Association, 2011).

6. Personal interview with Eric Nadelstern, New York City, December 15, 2011.

7. The 2001 RFP also invited proposals for whole-school reform of large comprehensive high schools. Since grants awarded for this purpose did not result in significant changes in the quality of education provided in the relevant schools, this option was eliminated from the RFPs in subsequent years. Personal interview with Robert Hughes, New York City, July 11, 2011.

8. Michael C. Rubenstein et al., *New Century High Schools: Evaluation Findings from the Second Year* (Washington, D.C.: Policy Studies Inc., 2005).

9. Page 7 of the application submitted by East Side House and its collaborators for a Bronx New Century High School. Josué Rodriguez of East Side House provided us with a copy of the application.

10. Mismatches between student needs and school structure are described in J. Eccles et al., "Development During Adolescence: The Impact of Stage-Environment Fit on Young Adolescents' Experiences in Schools and Families," *American Psychologist* 48 (1993): 90–101.

11. Personal interview with SLJ Principal Shannon Curran and Assistant Principal Suzette Dyer on March 13, 2013.

12. Personal interview with Eric Nadelstern, New York City, December 15, 2011.

13. Telephone interview on July 24, 2012, with Irma Zardoya and Pamela Ferner, who are respectively the president and the executive vice president of national initiatives for the New York City Leadership Academy.

14. The support networks run by nonprofit organizations are called Partnership Support Organizations (PSOs).

15. The Klein administration also supported the opening of many small high schools that do have admission requirements.

16. In the interest of full disclosure, we point out that Richard Murnane is a member of the MDRC Board of Directors.

17. The evaluation took advantage of the city's high school admissions process, which used a lottery-like mechanism to randomly assign students to those small schools of choice that

had more applicants than spaces. The evaluation team used a method known as instrumental variables to estimate the impact of enrolling in a small school of choice. It is described in Howard S. Bloom, Saskia Levy Thompson, and Rebecca Unterman, *Transforming the High School Experience: How New York City's New Small Schools Are Boosting Student Achievement and Graduation Rates* (New York: MDRC, 2010). An informative update to the evidence in the first report is provided in Howard S. Bloom and Rebecca Unterman, *Sustained Positive Effects on Graduation Rates Produced by New York City's Small Public High Schools of Choice* (New York City: MDRC Policy Brief, 2012).

18. The two sets of five-year graduation rates were 75.2% and 68.1%, respectively. The corresponding four-year graduation rates were 68.1% and 61.9%, respectively. The percentage of lottery winners who passed the state Regents English examination with a grade of 75 or higher was 37.3% as compared with 29.7% of lottery losers. For details, see Bloom, Thompson, and Unterman, *Transforming the High School Experience* (2010). As the appendix to the MDRC 2010 report explains, the evaluation methodology was quite complicated. One reason is that a student who lost a lottery for admission to one small school of choice might have won a lottery to another school of choice that he had rated lower on the list of high schools he would like to attend.

19. Small schools of choice and their partners have attempted to raise private funds to supplement public funding. For example, SLJ's advisory board took the unusual and aggressive step of creating a not-for-profit foundation to facilitate fundraising. Currently, the Adams Street Foundation raises over half a million dollars for SLJ, which the school uses to pay for summer enrichment programs and college visits along with the staff that makes these things happen. While all small schools of choice seek to raise private funds to provide the experiences and enrichment opportunities that affluent parents provide to their children, the schools vary in the degree to which they have been successful in doing so.

20. Another approach with a proven track record is the career academy, which is a small learning community embedded within a larger high school. Students in career academies take classes together for at least three years and are taught be a small group of teachers. The classes amount to a college-preparatory curriculum with a career theme that integrates academic and career technical education. Partnerships with local employers provide work-based learning opportunities. A carefully designed experimental evaluation of nine career academies showed that they boosted the labor market success of their students. Among students who participated in a lottery that allocated offers of a place in a career academy, those who won offers had labor market earnings eight years after graduation that were 11% higher, on average, than students who lost out in one of the lotteries. See Kemple, *Career Academies* (2008).

21. "*Horace* Talks with Eric Nadelstern: New York City's Autonomy Zone," 2005. Available in December 2011 at http://www.essentialschools.org/resources/312.

22. Robert Balfanz et al., *Building a Grad Nation: Progress and Challenge in Ending the High School Dropout Epidemic* (Baltimore, MD: Civic Enterprises, Everyone Graduates Center at Johns Hopkins University, 2012).

23. Elizabeth A. City, *Resourceful Leadership: Tradeoffs and Tough Decisions on the Road to School Improvement* (Cambridge, MA: Harvard Education Press, 2008), 192.

24. Economist Henry Levin estimates that interventions that result in a disadvantaged youth graduating from high school who otherwise would not have done so saves the public $209,100 (in 2004 dollars), or adjusting for inflation, $254,840 in 2012 prices. The MDRC estimate is that out of every 100 disadvantaged youth who desired to enroll in a small

school of choice, seven graduated who would not have done so had they not been able to enroll in a small school of choice. Making the conservative estimate that enrollment in a small school of choice brought benefits only to those seven students who graduated as a result of their enrollment in a small school, the present value of the total public savings of providing small schools of choice for four years for the 100 students is $1,783,880, calculated as $254,840 × 7. Dividing by 100 produces an average public benefit of $17,839 from the investment of providing a better four-year high school education for the 100 students. Dividing by 4 produces an annual per student cost of $4,460. This is admittedly a very rough calculation. It does not include as benefits the present value of the extra earnings, net of taxes, that youth earned over a lifetime as a result of graduating from high school. The source of the $209,100 public benefit figure is as follows: Henry M. Levin, "The Economic Payoff to Investing in Educational Justice," *Educational Researcher* 38, no. 1 (2009): 5–20.

Chapter 8

1. These associations have been repeatedly confirmed in the research literature. A recent example showing these patterns in both the United States and the United Kingdom is Paula Fomby, Shannon Cavanagh, and Joshua Goode, *Family Instability and School Readiness in the United States and the United Kingdom* (National Center for Family and Marriage Research Working Paper Series, WP-11-06, Bowling Green State University, Nov. 2011).

2. Robert Wood, Quinn Moore, Andrew Clarkwest, Alexandra Killewald, and Shannon Monahan, *The Long-Term Effects of Building Strong Families: A Relationship Skills Education Program for Unmarried Parents* (Executive Summary, OPRE Report # 2012-28B, Washington, D.C.: Office of Planning, Research and Evaluation, Administration for Children and Families, U.S. Department of Health and Human Services, 2012).

3. A recent review of this evidence is provided in Douglas Kirby and B. A. Laris, "Effective Curriculum-Based Sex and STD/HIV Education Programs for Adolescents," *Child Development Perspectives* 3 (2009): 21–29. It finds no evidence that abstinence-only programs delay sexual onset or in other ways affect sexual behavior, but programs combining abstinence with contraceptives including condoms often did produce measurable positive impacts on sexual behavior.

4. A recent review of this literature is provided in Gayle Hamilton and Susan Scrivener, *Facilitating Postsecondary Education and Training for TANF Recipients* (Temporary Assistance for Needy Families Program Research Synthesis Brief Series, Urban Institute, March 2012).

5. Frank Furstenberg, "The Challenges of Finding Causal Links Between Family Educational Practices and Schooling Outcomes," in *Whither Opportunity? Rising Inequality, Schools, and Children's Life Chances*, eds. Greg J. Duncan and Richard J. Murnane (New York: Russell Sage Foundation and the Spencer Foundation, 2011), 465–482.

6. See Ron Haskins, *Work Over Welfare: The Inside Story of the 1996 Welfare Reform Law* (Washington, D.C.: Brookings Institution, 2006), and Jason DeParle, *American Dream: Three Women, Ten Kids, and a Nation's Drive to End Welfare* (New York: Penguin Books, 2005), for political histories of welfare reform.

7. This description of Inez in particular and the New Hope program in general follows those provided in Greg Duncan, Aletha Huston, and Thomas Weisner, *Higher Ground: New Hope for the Working Poor and Their Children* (New York: Russell Sage, 2007). Inez and the names of other family members are the pseudonyms used in that book.

8. Haskins (2006) and DeParle (2005).

9. In 2012 dollars, the $1,384 credit in 1992 translates into $2,264.

10. Irene Lurie, *At the Front Lines of the Welfare System* (Albany, NY: Rockefeller Institute Press, 2006).

11. Johannes Bos, Aletha Huston, Robert Granger, Greg Duncan, Thomas Brock, and Vonnie McLoyd, in *New Hope for People with Low Incomes: Two-Year Results of a Program to Reduce Poverty and Reform Welfare* (New York: MDRC, 1999), provide details on the design and early impacts of New Hope. This description draws from Johannes Bos, Greg Duncan, Lisa Gennetian, and Heather Hill, *New Hope: Fulfilling America's Promise to "Make Work Pay"* (Hamilton Project Paper, Washington, D.C.: Brookings Institution, 2007).

12. In 2012 dollars, $12.50 translates into $15.20.

13. Duncan, Huston, and Weisner (2007) provide the most general summary of New Hope's impacts. "Earnings" here include income from all jobs, including New Hope's community service jobs. New Hope's earnings supplements are *not* included in these earnings amounts.

14. Data on the differential impacts of the program depending on the initial employment status of the participants are presented in Aletha C. Huston, Cynthia Miller, Lashawn Richburg-Hayes, Greg J. Duncan, Carolyn A. Eldred, Thomas S. Weisner, Edward Lowe, Vonnie C. McLoyd, Danielle A. Crosby, Marika N. Ripke, and Cindy Redcross, *New Hope for Families and Children: Five-Year Results of a Program to Reduce Poverty and Reform Welfare* (New York: MDRC, 2003).

15. Jennifer Romich, "Trying to keep children out of trouble: Child characteristics, neighborhood quality, and within-household resource allocation," *Children and Youth Services Review* 31, no. 3 (2009): 338–345.

16. Aletha C. Huston, Anjali E. Gupta, Jessica Thornton Walker, Chantelle Dowsett, Sylvia R. Epps, Amy Imes, and Vonnie C. McLoyd, "The long-term effects on children and adolescents of a policy providing work supports for low-income parents," *Journal of Policy Analysis and Management* 30, no. 4 (2011):729–754, and Cynthia Miller, Aletha C. Huston, Greg J. Duncan, Vonnie C. McLoyd, Thomas S. Weisner, *New Hope for the Working Poor: Effects After Eight Years for Families and Children* (New York: MDRC, 2008).

17. It is tricky to think about the policy implications of results from a follow-up conducted five years after the end of the program. Although tested as a three-year program, New Hope creators had intended that New Hope (like the Earned Income Tax Credit) would provide ongoing rather than time-limited benefits as long as families met New Hope's 30-hour-per-week work requirement.

18. This analysis is presented in Huston et al. (2003).

19. Bos et al. (2007, p. 17) discuss how New Hope might be scaled up in different states. They suggest that the "program be administered by existing state and local agencies and not-for-profit organizations. Depending on the specific infrastructure in each state, New Hope services could be delivered through the workforce development system, a health maintenance system, county public assistance agencies, or a network of not-for-profit agencies. In a large state, the program could use a combination of these delivery systems tailored to the specific infrastructure of local areas."

20. David Hage, in *Reforming Welfare by Rewarding Work* (Minneapolis: University of Minnesota Press, 2004), provides a comprehensive history of the development of the Minnesota program and its evaluation.

21. The picture was more mixed for people newly applying for welfare. Those in the Family Investment Program worked more but, because they sometimes took part-time jobs, earned less than their comparison-group counterparts. Their incomes were higher and poverty was reduced because of the earnings supplement, but their children were not doing better,

and, on some measures, were performing less well in school. For an evaluation of MFIP's implementation, see Patricia Auspos, Jo Hunter, Virginia Knox, Cynthia Miller, and Alan Orenstein, *Making Work and Welfare Pay: Implementation and 18-month Impacts of the Minnesota Family Investment Program* (New York: MDRC, 1997).

22. Lisa Gennetian and Cynthia Miller, *Reforming Welfare and Rewarding Work: Final Report on the Minnesota Family Investment Program*, vol. 2, *Effects on Children* (New York: MDRC, 2000). As documented in Anna Gassman-Pines and Hirokazu Yoshikawa, "Five-Year Effects of an Anti-Poverty Program on Marriage Among Never-Married Mothers," *Journal of Policy Analysis and Management* 25, no. 1 (2006): 11–30, New Hope also had positive impacts on marriage but did not ask about domestic violence. Other studies have found less positive effects of welfare reform policies that require work among recent applicants for welfare compared with those who were long-term recipients. Among the many possible reasons are that recent applicants are often in a crisis from divorce or job loss that may interfere with their ability to be employed, and many will find jobs and leave welfare whether or not it is tied to work requirements (see Marty Zaslow, Kristen Moore, Jennifer Brooks, Pamela Morris, Katherine Tout, Zakia Redd, and Carol Emig, "Experimental Studies of Welfare Reform and Children," *Future of Children* 12, no. 1 (2002): 79–98.

23. The Minnesota program boosted formal but not informal child-care use; see Lisa Gennetian, Greg Duncan, Virginia Knox, Wanda Vargas, Elizabeth Clark-Kauffman, and Andrew London, "How Welfare Policies Can Affect Adolescents: A Synthesis of Evidence from Experimental Studies," *Journal of Research on Adolescence* 14 (2004): 399–423.

24. Gennetian and Miller, *Reforming Welfare and Rewarding Work* (2000).

25. Bos et al., *New Hope: Fulfilling America's Promise* (2007). A roughly equal amount of money was spent on the payment of benefits provided to participants, but since those costs to taxpayers constitute benefits for participants, a social accounting of program costs considers them a wash, leaving the social cost at $2,000 (in 2012 dollars).

26. Derek Neal and William Johnson, "The Role of Premarket Factors in Black-White Wage Differences," *Journal of Political Economy* 104, no. 5 (1996): 869–895, and David Anderson, "The Aggregate Burden of Crime," *Journal of Law and Economics* 42, no. 2 (1999): 611–642.

27. Most of this amount goes to the children themselves. This is a societal benefit, reflecting their increased work productivity. About $300 of the total accrues to taxpayers in the form of higher taxes paid.

28. The logic of this calculation is spelled out in Bos et al. (2007). We repeat the earlier point about the difficulty in thinking about impacts five years after the end of a program, when that program's eventual design was intended to provide ongoing, as opposed to time-limited, benefits to qualifying families.

29. Scott E. Carrell and Mark L. Hoekstra, "Externalities in the Classroom: How Children Exposed to Domestic Violence Affect Everyone's Kids," *American Economic Journal: Applied Economics* 2, no. 1 (Jan. 2010): 211–228.

30. Gordon B. Dahl and Lance Lochner, "The Impact of Family Income on Child Achievement: Evidence from the Earned Income Tax Credit," *American Economic Review* 102 (2012): 1927–1956, and Williams Evans and Craig Garthwaite, "Giving mom a break: The impact of higher EITC payments on maternal health" (NBER Working Paper No. 16296, Cambridge, MA: National Bureau of Economic Research, 2010). See chapter 3 for some details about these studies.

31. See, for example, Laura Snyder, Robin Rudowitz, Rachel Garfield, and Tracy Gordon, *Why Does Medicaid Spending Vary Across States: A Chart Book of Factors Driving State Spending*

(Kaiser Commission on Medicaid and the Uninsured, Nov. 2012), http://www.kff.org/medicaid/upload/8378.pdf, and *Administration of Children and Families: The CCDF Policies Database Book of Tables: Key Cross-State Variations*, in CCDF Policies As of October 1, 2011, http://www.acf.hhs.gov/sites/default/files/opre/ccdf_policies_database_2011_book_of_tables.pdf.

Chapter 9

1. Greg J. Duncan and Richard J. Murnane, "Introduction: The American Dream Then and Now" in *Whither Opportunity?*, eds. Duncan and Murnane (2011), 3–23.
2. Tim R. Sass et al., *Value Added of Teachers in High-Poverty Schools and Lower Poverty Schools* (Washington, D.C.: CALDER working paper no. 52, Urban Institute, 2010).
3. See, for example, Howard S. Becker, "The Career of the Chicago Public School Teacher," *American Journal of Sociology* 57, no. 5 (1952): 470–477.
4. Sheila E. Murray, William N. Evans, and Robert M. Schwab, "Education-Finance Reform and the Distribution of Education Resources," *American Economic Review* 88, no. 4 (Sept. 1998): 789–812.
5. Nora Gordon, "Do Federal Grants Boost School Spending? Evidence from Title I," *Journal of Public Economics* 88, no. 9–10 (Aug. 2004) 1771-1792; Elizabeth U. Cascio, Nora E. Gordon, and Sarah J. Reber, "Local Responses to Federal Grants: Evidence from the Introduction of Title I in the South," *American Economic Journal: Economic Policy* 5, no. 3 (August 2013): 126–159.
6. Marvin H. Kosters and Brent D. Mast, *Closing the Education Achievement Gap: Is Title I Working?* (Washington, D.C.: AEI Press, 2003); Geoffrey D. Borman and Jerome V. Agostino, "Title I and Student Achievement: A Meta-Analysis of Federal Evaluation Results," *Educational Evaluation and Policy Analysis* 18, no. 4 (1996).
7. Marguerite Roza, *Educational Economics: Where Do School Funds Go?* (Washington, D.C.: Urban Institute Press, 2010); Jacob E. Adams, *Smart Money: Using Educational Resources to Accomplish Ambitious Learning Goals* (Cambridge, MA: Harvard Education Press, 2010).
8. Richard F. Elmore, *School Reform from the Inside Out: Policy, Practice, and Performance* (Cambridge, MA: Harvard Education Press, 2004).
9. See, for example, Chetty et al., *How Does Your Kindergarten Classroom*; Raj Chetty, John N. Friedman, and Jonah H. Rockoff, *The Long-Term Impacts of Teachers: Teacher Value-Added and Student Outcomes in Adulthood* (working paper no. 17699, National Bureau of Economic Research, Cambridge, MA: 2011); Richard J. Murnane, John B. Willett, and Frank Levy, "The Growing Importance of Cognitive Skills in Wage Determination," *Review of Economics and Statistics* 77, no. 2 (1995).
10. Thomas S. Dee and Brian Jacob, "The Impact of No Child Left Behind on Student Achievement," *Journal of Policy Analysis and Management* 30, no. 3 (July 2011): 418–446.
11. Richard J. Murnane and John P. Papay, "Teachers' Views on No Child Left Behind: Support for the Principles, Concerns about the Practices," *Journal of Economic Perspectives* 24, no. 3 (July 2010).
12. Ibid.
13. Derek Neal and Diane Whitmore Schanzenbach, "Left Behind by Design: Proficiency Counts and Test-Based Accountability," *Review of Economics and Statistics* 92, no. 2 (May 2010): 263–283.
14. Brian Jacob and Steven Levitt, "Rotten Apples: An Investigation of the Prevalence and Predictors of Teacher Cheating," *Quarterly Journal of Economics* 118, no. 3 (2003): 843–877.

15. Michele McNeil, "States Punch Reset Button with NCLB Waivers," *Education Week*, 32, no. 8 (Oct. 17, updated Nov. 19, 2012).

16. John E. Chubb and Terry M. Moe, *Politics, Markets and America's Schools* (Washington, D.C.: Brookings, 1990).

17. Stacey M. Childress, Denis P. Doyle, and David A. Thomas, in *Leading for Equity: The Pursuit of Excellence in Montgomery County Public Schools* (Cambridge, MA: Harvard Education Press, 2009), present evidence on the results of an alternative model for improving the performance of a large school district in educating children from low-income families.

18. Charles M. Payne, *So Much Reform, So Little Change: The Persistence of Failure in Urban Schools* (Cambridge, MA: Harvard Education Press, 2008).

19. Chubb and Moe, *Politics, Markets and America's Schools.*

20. Caroline M. Hoxby, "Does Competition Among Public Schools Benefit Students and Taxpayers?" *American Economic Review* 90, no. 5 (2000): 1209–1238; Caroline M. Hoxby, *How School Choice Affects the Achievement of Public School Students* (paper prepared for the Koret Task Force meeting on Sept. 20–21, Hoover Institution, Stanford, CA, 2001).

21. Critics of charter schools point to several ways in which they do not compete on an even playing field with conventional public schools. One is that relatively few learning-disabled students and English language learners apply to charter schools. Consequently, a disproportionate number of these children, who are expensive to educate, end up in conventional public schools. Supporters of charter schools point out that schools typically receive extra funds for serving children with special needs that they can use on resources to support these children and to deal with behavioral disruptions. They also argue that a consistently enforced schoolwide code of behavior, a coherent plan of instruction, and rapid intervention to support struggling students go a long way in solving the discipline problems that plague many conventional public schools. Finally, supporters argue that many charter schools do not receive as much funding per student as the conventional public schools with which they compete. For a thoughtful brief review of the evidence on charter schools, see Julian R. Betts and Richard C. Atkinson, "Better Research Needed on the Impact of Charter Schools," *Science* 335, no. 6065 (2012): 171–172.

22. Ibid.; Steven F. Wilson, "Success at Scale in Charter Schooling" (working paper 2008-02, AEI Future of American Education Project, American Enterprise Institute, Washington, D.C., 2008).

23. Chubb and Moe, *Politics, Markets and America's Schools.*

24. William G. Howell and Paul E. Peterson, *The Education Gap: Vouchers and Urban Schools*, rev. ed. (Washington, D.C.: Brookings Institution Press, 2006), 323. Evidence of effects of the New York Scholarship Program has weakened over time. The original work by Howell and Peterson (2002) found positive effects for African American families on math achievement that persisted for three years, but not for Hispanic families. Alan Krueger and P. Zhu, in "Another look at the New York City school voucher experiment," *American Behavioral Scientist* 47 (2004), 658–698, show that these results are sensitive to the classification of the child's race as African American. Moreover, Marianne P. Bitler, Thurston Domina, Emily K. Penner, and Hilary W. Hoynes, in *Distributional Effects of a School Voucher Program: Evidence from New York City* (University of California, Irvine, working paper, 2013), identified a coding error in the test scores used in both of the preceding papers that further changed the results.

25. For the evidence on New Zealand, see Edward B. Fiske and Helen F. Ladd, *When Schools Compete: A Cautionary Tale* (Washington, D.C.: Brookings, 2000). For the evidence on

Chile, see Patrick J. McEwan, Miguel Urquiola, and Emiliana Vegas, "School Choice, Strati-fication, and Information on School Performance: Lessons from Chile," *Economia: Journal of the Latin American and Caribbean Economic Association* 8, no. 2 (Spring 2008): 1–27, 38–42.

26. National Governors Association Center for Best Practices and Council of Chief State School Officers, *Common Core State Standards* (Washington, D.C.: NGACBP, CCSSO, 2010).

27. For example, the evidence Professor Douglas Clements of the University of Denver gath-ered over many years about the development of preschool math skills informed the overall approach and the details of the Building Blocks curriculum. As an illustration, see Douglas H. Clements and Julie Sarama, "Experimental Evaluation of the Effects of a Research-Based Preschool Mathematics Curriculum," *American Educational Research Journal* 45 (2008): 443–494.

28. For information on advances in understanding of children's development of reading skills and the impacts of the research on curricula, see the articles on literacy challenges for the 21st century in Richard J. Murnane, Catherine E. Snow, and Isabel V. Sawhill, eds., *The Future of Children* 22, no. 2 (2012).

29. New Visions for Public Schools, *New Century High Schools for New York City Initiative: Re-quest for Proposals* (NVPS, New York, 2001). This documents spells it out in the following way: "Success in the 21st century requires mastery of high school level mathematics, writ-ten and oral communications skills, and the ability to solve problems, work as a member of a team, and use technology. The preservation of democracy in a diverse country demands that schools give children and youth experiences and knowledge that will build the civic competencies of tolerance, inter-group communication, conflict resolution, and engage-ment in public life . . . Research on resiliency identifies environmental factors that greatly increase the chances for academic and social success of youth living in high risk environ-ments. These factors are caring relationships with adults who have high expectations of them; participation in activities that engage their voluntary commitment; opportunities to make contributions and to have these recognized and assessed; and continuity of support."

30. Benjamin L. Castleman and Lindsay C. Page, "A Trickle or a Torrent? Understanding the Extent of Summer 'Melt' among College-Intending High School Graduates," *Social Science Quarterly* (2013): 1–19; Benjamin L. Castleman, Karen Arnold, and Katherine Lynk Wart-man, "Stemming the Tide of Summer Melt: An Experimental Study of the Effects of Post-High School Summer Intervention on Low-Income Students' College Enrollment," *Journal of Research on Educational Effectiveness* 5, no. 1 (2012): 1–17.

31. Greg J. Duncan, Aletha Huston, and Tom Weisner, *Higher Ground: New Hope for the Work-ing Poor and Their Children* (New York: Russell Sage, 2007).

32. Patricia Albjerg Graham, *Schooling America: How the Public Schools Meet the Nation's Changing Needs* (Oxford: Oxford University Press, 2005).

33. Golden and Katz, *Race Between Education and Technology* (2008).

34. Douglas N. Harris, "High Flying Schools, Student Disadvantage, and the Logic of NCLB," *American Journal of Education* 113, no. 3 (2007): 367–394.

35. This argument is developed in Greg J. Duncan and Richard J. Murnane, "Introduction: The American Dream, Then and Now," in *Whither Opportunity? Rising Inequality, Schools, and Children's Life Chances*, eds. Greg J. Duncan and Richard J. Murnane (New York: Russell Sage Foundation and Spencer Foundation, 2011), and in several other chapters in this volume.

36. Susan M. Johnson, Matthew A. Kraft, and John P. Papay, "How Context Matters in High-Need Schools: The Effects of Teachers' Working Conditions on Their Professional Satisfaction and Their Students' Achievement," *Teachers College Record* 114, no. 10 (2012); Helen F. Ladd, "Teachers' Perceptions of Their Working Conditions: How Predictive of Planned and Actual Teacher Movement?" *Educational Evaluation and Policy Analysis* 33, no. 2 (June 2011): 235–261.
37. Goldin and Katz, *Race Between Education and Technology* (2008).
38. Ibid.

Acknowledgments

This book is the second product of a six-year research project examining the ways in which increases in family income inequality in the United States have affected the educational opportunities of children growing up in low-income families. That project was initiated by Rebecca Blank, who brought scholars together under the auspices of the Russell Sage and Spencer Foundations to brainstorm about the design of a major research effort to increase knowledge in this area. Richard Murnane was asked to cochair the emerging project. When Blank entered government service in 2009, Greg Duncan agreed to join Murnane in leading the research effort. The first product, *Whither Opportunity? Rising Inequality, Schools, and Children's Life Chances* (The Russell Sage and Spencer Foundations, 2011), edited by Duncan and Murnane, summarizes evidence collected by fifty-one scholars on trends in the educational outcomes of children from low- and higher-income families, and on the ways in which families, schools, and neighborhoods affect children's life chances.

The response to *Whither Opportunity?* was gratifying. The volume was reviewed favorably by scholars and generated significant media attention. However, because its target audience was the research community, we were concerned that legislators, school committee members, educators, and the many other leaders and practitioners whose work affects children would not learn about the new evidence that had been gathered. A second concern was that the volume focused on diagnosis, not prescription. Many readers and representatives of the media asked us: In the face of growing family income inequality, what should be done to improve the life chances of children growing up in low-income families? This book is intended to address these two concerns—explaining the problem to a wider audience and identifying promising policy responses.

Our discussions of possible interventions are based on evidence from quantitative-impact evaluations that were conducted using cutting-edge methodologies. But rather than merely presenting that evidence, we wanted to bring these ideas to life for our readers. We therefore visited classrooms to observe teachers and students at the sites of the interventions, and we interviewed program developers, educators, parents, and students. We asked about the strengths and limitations of the interventions, how those interventions affected them personally, and the obstacles they saw to providing such promising programs to more children and families. We are deeply indebted to the great many people who answered our questions and allowed us to observe their work.

At the risk of inadvertently omitting some names, we want to thank individuals who contributed to this book in a variety of ways. Key sources of information on the Boston preK program included Jason Sachs, the director of Early Childhood Education for the Boston Public Schools (BPS); Emily Cox, the principal of the Mather Elementary School; Marina Boni, a BPS preschool coach; and Christina Weiland, who led the research team that evaluated the program.

In the course of studying the University of Chicago Charter School network, we learned a great deal from conversations with Tim Knowles, director of the University's Urban Education Institute (UEI); Molly Branson Thayer and Shayne Evans of the UEI staff; Stephen Raudenbush, the lead program evaluator; Tanika Island-Smith, the principal of North Kenwood/Oakland (NKO), one of the charter school campuses in the network; and four NKO teachers: Erica Emmendorfer, Shannon Keys, Sarah Nowak, and Carrie Walsh.

As we sought to learn more about the small schools of choice initiative in New York City, we benefited from conversations with Michele Cahill, vice president of the Carnegie Corporation of New York; Robert Hughes, president of New Visions for Public Schools; New Visions staff members Jennie Soler-McIntosh and Ron Chulaison; Richard Kahan, CEO of the Urban Assembly; Urban Assembly staff member Jennifer Ostrow; Saskia Levy Thompson, special advisor to the Chancellor of the New York City Public Schools; James Kemple, executive director of the Research Alliance for New York City Schools; Josué Rodriguez, associate executive director of the East Side House Settlement; Eric Nadelstern, who served as chief academic officer for the Office of New Schools in the New York City Public Schools; Ana Maldonado and Flavia Puello Perdomo, principals of Mott Haven Village Preparatory High School; Shannon Curran, principal of the Urban Assembly School for Law and Justice (SLJ); and SLJ teachers Suzette Dyer and Eyal Wallenberg.

Among those who provided helpful comments on drafts of chapters and/or answered questions on specific topics were Ana Auger, David Autor, Gordon Berlin, Katherine Boles, Barnie Brawer, Cynthia Brown, Jeron Campbell, Elizabeth City, David Cohen, Thurston Domina, Nora Gordon, Patricia Graham, Ellen Guiney, Ron Haskins, Marvin Hoffman, Kari Kokka, Frank Levy, Erica Litke, Jal Mehta, Joseph Pinto, Sean Reardon, Sarah Reber, Nicole Simon, Catherine Snow, Rebecca Unterman, Christina Weiland, and Hiro Yoshikawa. Special thanks go to Annette Lareau, who provided extensive comments and other assistance on the material we drew from her book *Unequal Childhoods*, and to Tracy Kidder for the vivid portrayals of teaching we drew from his book *Among Schoolchildren*.

We would also like to thank David Autor, Claudia Goldin, and Sean Reardon for providing data, Kathleen Ziol-Guest and Sabino Kornrich for data analysis, Wendy Angus for keeping track of multiple versions of the manuscript, and Kathleen Donovan and Carla Lillvik for expert advice on references and library matters.

We are deeply grateful to Michael McPherson, president of the Spencer Foundation, and Eric Wanner, president of the Russell Sage Foundation, for their support for this project from the outset and for the funding that made it possible. They and their colleagues, Diana Hess from the Spencer Foundation and Suzanne Nichols from the Russell Sage Foundation, as well as several anonymous reviewers, read many drafts of the manuscript and pushed us to make it better. We also thank Caroline Chauncey, our editor at Harvard Education Press, and Barbara Ray, of HiredPen.com, for their magnificent editorial work.

Finally, we would like to thank our wives, Dorothy Duncan and Mary Jo Murnane, whose support, encouragement, and, in Dorothy's case, extensive editorial comments, made completion of the book possible.

About the Authors

Greg J. Duncan is Distinguished Professor in the School of Education at the University of California, Irvine. With a 1974 PhD in economics, Duncan spent the first two decades of his career at the University of Michigan working on, and ultimately directing, the Panel Study of Income Dynamics (PSID) data collection project, which, in 2001, was named by the National Science Foundation to be one of the fifty most significant NSF-funded projects in the organization's history. Beginning in the late 1980s, Duncan engaged in a number of interdisciplinary research networks and began to focus on the impacts of family and neighborhood conditions on children's cognitive and behavioral development. During his 1995–2008 tenure at Northwestern University, he was the Edwina S. Tarry Professor in the School of Education and Social Policy. He coauthored *Higher Ground: New Hope for the Working Poor and Their Children* (2007) and coedited *Neighborhood Poverty* (1997), *Consequences of Growing Up Poor* (1997) and, most recently, *Whither Opportunity? Rising Inequality, Schools, and Children's Life Chances* (2011). He was president of the Midwest Economics Association in 2004, the Population Association of America in 2008, and the Society for Research in Child Development (2009–2011). Duncan was elected to the National Academy of Sciences in 2010.

Richard J. Murnane, an economist, is the Thompson Professor at the Harvard Graduate School of Education (HGSE). He is also a research associate at the National Bureau of Economic Research, a Fellow of the Society of Labor Economists, and a member of the American Academy of Arts and Sciences. Before earning his PhD in economics from Yale University, Murnane taught high school mathematics for three years. In recent years he has pursued three lines of research. With MIT professors Frank Levy and David Autor, he has examined how computer-based technological change has affected skill demands in the U.S. economy, and the effectiveness of educational policies in responding to changing skill demands. Murnane and Levy have written two books on this topic. The second line of research examines the sources of the growing gap in educational outcomes between children from low-income and higher-income families and the effectiveness of alternative strategies for improving the life chances low-income children. Murnane coedited (with Greg Duncan) the 2011 volume *Whither Opportunity? Rising Inequality, Schools, and Children's Life Chances.* The third line of research focuses on examining trends and patterns in U.S. high school graduation rates and their explanations. Murnane's summary of the evidence on this topic was published in the June 2013 issue of the *Journal of Economic Literature.* In 2011 Murnane and his colleague John Willett published the book *Methods Matter: Improving Causal Inference in Educational and Social Science Research.*

Index

Abecedarian Project, 56–57, 67
absent fathers, 29
abstinence-based high school sex programs,
    109
academic achievement
    domestic violence and, 47
    English language learners, 48–49
    gaps between high- and low-income
        children, 2, 16, 67
    residential isolation, 41–51
    student mobility, 47–48
    Title I funds, 127–128
academic standards, 51
    preparing students to meet higher, 141
    rising, 37–41
accountability, 4, 5
    American education, 136–138
    Common Core-based assessments, 137
    high-poverty schools, 84
    low-income children, 137
    North Kenwood/Oakland (NKO) campus,
        84
    schools, 50, 52, 136–138
    supports, 52, 137
    teachers, 137
    test-based accountability, 128–130
    well-designed, 52, 137
Achievement First, 80, 131
achievement gaps, 2
    Boston Public Schools (BPS), 58–59
    high-poverty schools, 42
    income inequality, 26
    low-income children, 58
    low-poverty schools, 42

administrators
    manipulating students' test scores, 129
    view of small high schools, 87
adolescents
    completing more education than parents, 20
    development and skills, 138–139
    self-perceptions, 92
    transition from childhood to, 92
American education
    accountability, 136–138
    advances in knowledge, 138–139
    building blocks for solution, 133–140
    commission examining, 38
    Common Core State Standards, 133–134
    educational choices, 132
    meeting challenge, 140–144
    nineteenth century leadership in, 143
    supporting families in ways that help
        children, 139–140
    supports and support organizations, 134,
        136
America's Choice, 82–83
Among Schoolchildren (Kidder), 35–36
A Nation at Risk, 38
Anneberg Challenge, 87, 88, 93
Annenberg Foundation, 87
Antigone (Sophocles), 95
Apollo Theater, 99
assessments, 51

Baker, Ashanti, 86, 94, 104
balanced literacy, 40–41
Baltimore public schools, 82

behavioral problems, 27–28
  improvements reducing crime, 120–121
Bell, T.H., 38
Bloomberg, Michael, 99
blue-collar occupations, 13
Board of Education, 88
Boni, Marina, 56, 62–64, 66, 136, 137
Boot Camp, 4
Boston Globe, 59
Boston Public Schools (BPS)
  achievement gaps, 58–59
  Building Blocks mathematics curriculum,
    60
  "Building Communities" component, 60
  challenges, 66–67
  children from all backgrounds, 68
  classroom management, 62
  Department of Early Childhood (DEC), 54,
    59–61
  Early Childhood Learning Centers, 60
  educational supports for teachers, 61
  evaluation evidence, 65–66
  increasing funding for, 128
  language and literacy skills, 60
  low-income families, 58
  National Association for the Education
    of Young Children (NAEYC)
    accreditation, 64–65
  Opening the World of Learning (OWL)
    literacy curriculum, 60
  parents' work schedules, 67
  prekindergarten program, 59–60
  preschool education, 58–65
  professionals assisting teachers, 62
  qualified teachers, 66
  quality and consistency of instruction, 61
  quality improvement emphasis, 68–69
  staffing to implement curriculum, 61
  students acquiring skills and knowledge,
    65–66
  vocabulary and language skills, 64
Boston Teachers Residency Program, 136
Bronx Council on the Arts, 99
Brooklyn Law School, 98
Building Blocks mathematics curriculum, 60
"Building Communities" component, 60
Bush, George W., 129
Bushwick High School, 105

Cahill, Michele, 87, 88, 100, 138
Career and Technical Education high schools,
  105

Carnegie Corporation of New York, 87, 88
center-based child care and preschool, 119–120
Central Park East, 87
charter management organizations (CMOs),
  73, 81–82, 131–132
charter schools
  charter management organizations (CMOs),
    131–132
  closing ineffective, 79
  effectiveness, 78–80
  logistical challenges, 79
  low-income children, 79, 131
  management support for, 80
  no excuses model, 79
  not competing with public schools, 131
  regulations varying by state, 131
  school district practices, 131
  student skills improvement, 79
  supports to succeed, 131
  tasks facing, 79
  teachers and, 79
  unions contracts, 131
Chicago public school system, 45–46
  student mobility, 48
child care, center-based, 119–120
children
  circumstances shaping rest of life, 23
  cognitive and behavior problems, 27–28
  deficits of poverty, 27
  deprivation harm to, 27–28
  domestic violence and, 47
  enrichment gap, 139
  introducing new words, 53–54
  neighborhood schools, 41
  quickly falling behind, 124
  standard of living, 1
  success in school, 25
  supporting families in ways that help,
    139–140
Children First reform, 100
Children's First network, 102
class-related language differences, 32
classroom management
  high-poverty schools, 45–46
  strategies, 76
classrooms
  hurdles to reform, 5
  integrating new students, 47–48
  lack of consistency between, 76
  teacher's ability to control, 45
Clinton, Bill, 113
cognitive problems, 27–28
college, 15–16

access to, 8
affluent families, 17
graduates, 15
graduation rates, 17
growth in wages, 1
high- and low-income children gap, 17–18, 25
penalty for bypassing, 12
Common Core State Standards, 5, 38, 133–134
English language arts and mathematics,
134–135
information about children's mastery of
skills and knowledge, 134
mastering conceptual skills in, 126
tracking student scores, 144
comprehensive school reform design
organizations, 82–83
computer-based technological changes, 125
computer-driven technological advances, 1
computers, 9, 14
Contompasis, Michael, 59
Council of Supervisors and Administrators, 88
Cravath, Swaine & Moore LLP, 93
culture of continuous improvement, 141
Curran, Shannon, 96–97
curricula
aligning with standards, 51
not implemented appropriately, 41

Department of Early Childhood (DEC), 54,
59–61, 136
professional development, 62
technology for teaching lessons, 66–67
depression and school achievement, 28–30
Directory of the New York City Public High
Schools, 85
direct teacher-led instruction, 40
disadvantaged children
changes in secondary school education, 102
devoting more resources strategy, 126,
127–128
improving graduation rates, 106–107
improving high schools for, 107
meaningful improvement, 143
strategies for educating, 80
disruptive behavior and peers, 45–47
district administrative structures, 76
domestic violence, 47
Dyer, Suzette, 96

early childbearing, 29
early childhood, 54–58

brain development, 56
cognitive and language abilities, 55
education programs, 56
Earned Income Tax Credit (EITC) program,
29, 110, 113, 139–140
earnings, linking educational attainment to, 9
East Side House Settlement, 89–90, 136
afterschool program, 91
college preparation and leadership program,
97–98
human service programs, 98
economic growth, 1, 8
following World War II, 18
growth in education, 8
labor skills determining productivity, 15
economic inequality, 5
education
advances in knowledge, 138–139
disparities in, 2–3
equal opportunity and, 133
family income inequality and growing gap,
18–19
growth in, 8
intergenerational mobility and, 19–21
problems with, 37
recent improvement strategies, 126–133
students mastering skills, 75
twenty-first century challenges, 75–78
educational attainment
elements for getting ahead, 12–13
gaps, 2
linking to earnings, 9
needed to earn good living, 125
educational outcomes inequality, 3, 125–126
educators beating the odds, 141
effective teachers, 49–50
eighth grade gap between high- and low-
income children, 16
Elementary and Secondary Education Act
(1965), 127
elementary schools
student mobility, 48
successful, 71–84
elementary school teachers, 36
elements for getting ahead, 12–13
Emmendorfer, Erica, 71, 78, 81, 84
English language learners academic
achievement, 48–49
English skills
Common Core State Standards, 134–135
predicting labor-market success, 129
enrichment expenditures, 26–28
equal opportunity and education, 133

European upward economic mobility, 21
executive functioning, 55

factors determining success in schools, 24–25
failing schools, political problems when
    closing, 105–106
families
    programs supporting, 109–122
    quality of relationships, 28–30
    upward mobility, 123
    work-support programs, 139–140
family
    structure and school achievement, 31–33
family income
    children's schooling success, 121
    growing education gap, 18–19
    inequality, 17, 132, 139, 141
    public policy actions, 110
    segregation by, 132, 141
federal government and elements of New Hope
    program, 122
Food Stamps, 110, 140
French-Canadian immigrants, 35

gangs, 92
Gates Foundation, 88, 107
Great Society initiative, 57
Green Dot Public Schools, 80, 131

Hart, Betty, 31–32
Head Start, 57
high-income children
    academic skills gaps, 67
    basic skills mastery, 37
    computer-based technological changes and,
        125
    math and reading gaps, 24–25
    parents managing lives, 32–33
    peers, 42–47
    test scores, 16
high-income families
    academic skills of children, 58
    gap with lower-income families, 18–19
    investing in children's education, 125
    living standards of children, 1
    residential isolation, 41–51
    spending differences, 28
high-poverty schools
    accountability, 84

achievement problems, 42
attracting and retaining high-quality
    teachers, 144
building support for, 82–83
classroom management, 45–46
comprehensive designs to improve, 82–83
cost of success in, 142–143
differences in education in, 125
difficulties educating children, 141–142
effective teachers, 49–50
extended-day and extended-year programs,
    142
high teacher turnover, 50, 51, 83, 84, 142
lack physical safety, 50
large-scale improvement, 83
novice teachers, 51
paying teachers higher salaries, 82
short-term success of, 142
strategies to improve education, 74–75
stress of teaching in, 50
strong supports for, 84
teachers, 50, 83, 125
working conditions, 50, 84
high school diplomas, 10
    intergenerational mobility, 7–8
    low-income children, 39–40, 85
high school dropouts, 1
High School for Contemporary Arts, 98–99
high school graduates
    competing for service jobs, 10
    disadvantaged children, 107
    economic and demographic forces on
        earnings, 15
    going directly into labor market, 7
    high- *versus* low-income, 25
    male promising careers, 8
    New York City, 87
    routine tasks in work force, 9
    states increasing requirements for, 38
    wages, 1
    weak academic preparation, 16
high schools
    abstinence-based sex programs,
        109
    creation of good, 106
    designs, 87–88
    graduation rates, 2, 85
    improving life chances, 85–108
    Latino males, 85
    low graduation rates, 106
    low-income children, 85–86, 107
    replacing large with small, 87

high school students
    landmark study of (1972), 7–8
    passing Regents examination, 98
high-skilled occupations, 14
Holyoke, Massachusetts, 35–37
Holyoke school, 75
Hughes, Robert, 88, 89, 93, 138

Illinois Standards Achievement Test (ISAT), 73
immigrants
    children and academic achievement, 48–49
    low-income, 41
    low-skilled jobs, 15
    participation in civic life, 140
    patterns of, 41
improvement strategies
    devoting resources to disadvantaged
        students, 126, 127–128
    different organizational structures, 130–133
    disappointing results from, 126–133
    test-based accountability, 126, 128–130
income, linking to school achievement, 30–31,
        33, 41–42
income inequality
    high-quality education, 41
    intergenerational mobility, 20
instruction
    accessing excellent, 125–126
    path to better, 40
    results guiding improvement, 73
instructional achievement, 76
intellectual development, 27
intergenerational mobility, 1
    high school diplomas, 7–8
    income inequality, 20
    schooling and, 19–21
Irish immigrants, 35
Island-Smith, Tanika, 78, 81, 84

jobs
    literacy requirements, 40
    middle-class opportunities, 14
    well paying, 38
Johns Hopkins University, 82
Johnson, Lyndon, 57

Kahan, Richard, 93
Kane, Kristen, 100
Kelly Elementary School, 35–37

Kerksick, Julie, 113, 114
Keys, Shannon, 3–4, 5, 71, 84, 134, 136
Kidder, Tracy, 35–36, 37, 42
kindergarten, building academic skills before,
    55–56
Klein, Joel, 99–100, 130–131
knowledge and adolescent development and
    skills, 138–139
Knowles, Tim, 77–78

labor force
    completing college rewards, 15
    productivity of economy, 15
    stringent demands on schools, 38
language differences, 32
Lareau, Annette, 2–3, 24, 26, 32, 97
lead paint, 27
learning
    affected by achievement and behavior of
        classmates, 41–47
    union contracts, 77
literacy focus across grades, 73
The Little Red Hen Makes a Pizza, 53–54, 55,
    61, 63
lower-wage countries and outsourcing, 9–10
low-income children
    academic skills, 58, 67
    accountability systems, 137
    achievement gaps, 58
    background knowledge, 138
    basic skills mastery, 37
    black and Hispanic immigrants, 48–49
    charter schools, 79
    computer-based technological changes and,
        125
    effective teachers, 49–50
    excellent schools, 83–84
    exit examinations, 39–40
    family income gap, 41
    family structures, 31
    high schools, 85–86, 106
    improving life chances, 106, 133
    math and reading gaps, 24–25
    New York City, 87–108
    parents managing lives, 32–33
    peers, 42–47
    preparing to thrive in twenty-first century,
        75–78
    problem behavior, 41
    school financial needs for, 127–128
    segregation, 141

low-income children (*continued*)
  test scores, 16
  vocabulary, 138
  voucher programs, 132
low-income families
  academic skills of children, 58
  Boston Public Schools (BPS), 58
  difficulties helping children from, 2
  domestic violence, 47
  Earned Income Tax Credit, 113
  earning their way out of poverty, 110–111
  educational choices, 132
  factors associated with, 29
  gap with higher-income families, 18–19
  immigrants, 41
  improving life chances of children, 56
  income and school success, 30–31
  investing in children's education, 125
  learning opportunities, 139
  living standards of children, 1
  maternal education level, 57
  maternal mental health, 29
  moving, 41
  parental support for adolescents, 97
  programs supporting, 109–122
  residential isolation, 41–51
  residentially mobile, 48
  spending differences, 28
  work and family demands, 30
low-income neighborhoods and safety of urban
  teens, 92
low-income schools
  novice teachers, 49–50
  teachers, 41, 49–51, 77
low-skilled jobs and immigrants, 15

Maldonado, Ana, 90, 101
Mann, Horace, 33
manufacturing and outsourcing, 1
Massachusetts public schools, 38
Massachusetts State Department of Education,
  59
maternal education and IQ levels, 32
mathematics
  achievement gap, 16, 24–25
  Common Core State Standards, 134–135
  skills predicting labor-market success,
    129
Mather Elementary School, 53–54
McAlister, Harold, 26–27, 97, 123–124
MDRC, 103, 107, 114
Mears, Anthony, 10–11, 13, 23, 97, 123–124

Meier, Deborah, 87
Menino, Thomas, 58
microprocessor revolution, 9
middle-class schools incentives for teachers, 50
middle-income children
  parents managing lives, 32–33
  segregation, 141
Minnesota experiments with welfare reform,
  119
Minnesota Family Investment Program
  (MFIP), 119
Mott Haven Village Preparatory High School,
  86, 89–93, 136
  afterschool program, 90
  Ana Maldonado as first principal, 91
  caring, rigor, and opportunities, 91–92
  cutbacks in funding and activities, 104
  educational alternative, 92
  increasing funding for, 128
  internships and summer learning
    opportunities, 98
  ninth-grade curriculum, 93
  planning team, 90
  professional development, 102
  PSAT and SAT exams, 98
  school leaders, 104–105
  school report card, 101
  School Support Organization (SSO), 101
  students visiting colleges, 98
  summer melt research, 139
  teachers, 92, 104–105
moving and low-income families, 41

Nadelstern, Eric, 89, 91, 99, 100, 105–106
National Assessment of Educational Progress
  (NAEP), 37
National Association for the Education of
  Young Children (NAEYC), 64–65, 69,
  128, 137
national welfare reform legislation, 113
New Century High Schools, 87–99
  Career and Technical Education high
    schools, 105
  closing large schools, 89
  "college for all," 105
  core team, 88, 89
  design principles, 98–99
  evaluation evidence, 102–104
  funding and planning for new school, 88
  long-term relationship with teachers, 101
  matching ninth graders to specific schools,
    101

Mott Haven Village Preparatory High
School, 89–93
ongoing challenges, 104–106
reading skills, 94–97
responses to request for proposals (RFP),
88–89
School Support Organizations (SSOs),
101–102
student evaluation, 103
teachers and school leaders burnout,
104–105
themes, 98–99
unions, 88
Urban Assembly School for Law and Justice
(SLJ), 93–94
New Hope program, 30, 110–122
benefits while avoiding work-disincentive
effects, 139
boys and risky behavior, 121
boys school achievement scores, 117–118
child-care subsidies, 112
community service jobs, 116
costs and benefits, 112, 120–121
earnings supplements, 111
employment and earnings impacts, 115–116
families' use of program, 115
generalizing results, 118–120
girls school achievement scores, 117–118
health insurance subsidies, 112
impacts, 114–118
job coaching, 114
positive parenting, 118
poverty rates, 116
project representatives, 113–114
school achievement, 116–118
self reliance, 115
small scale of, 119
social behavior, 117–118
social contract, 113
two-generation program, 112
welfare reform, 112–114
work supports, 121–122, 140
New Leaders for New Schools, 136
New Visions for Public Schools, 88–90, 102, 136
New York City
Board of Education, 88
Department of Education, 101
high school designs, 87–88
high school graduation rates, 87
low-income students, 87–108
New Century High Schools, 87–99
Office of New Schools, 100
small public high schools, 87

New York City Leadership Academy, 81, 101,
136
New York City public schools
black and Hispanic immigrants, 48–49
Career and Technical Education high
schools, 105
"college for all," 105
disadvantaged children without high school
diploma, 107
elements for improving, 106
governance, 99
leadership preparation, 81
political problems when closing failing
schools, 105–106
reforming, 100
school report card system, 100–101
selecting high schools, 85–86
New York Scholarship Program, 132
New York State and schools passing Regents
examination, 98
No Child Left Behind Act (NCLB), 129–130,
137
no excuses model charter schools, 79
Nordic countries upward economic mobility,
21
North Kenwood/Oakland (NKO) campus,
71–72, 134, 136, 137
accountability, 84
advances in knowledge, 138
assessment of student's skills, 73
continuous improvement in teaching and
learning, 84
Illinois Standards Achievement Test (ISAT),
73
increasing funding for, 128
literacy across grades focus, 73
literacy coach and teachers, 81
lottery to select students, 73
management support for, 80
planning instruction, 81
public school regulations exemptions, 73
reading and mathematical skills, 74, 75
reading interview, 72
reading zone, 72–73
results guiding instructional improvement,
73
stipends to teachers assuming additional
responsibilities, 81–82
Strategic Teaching and Evaluation of
Progress (STEP), 71–72
Study Island software, 72
Tanika Island-Smith leading, 78, 81
targeting remediation, 81, 83

novice teachers, 49–51
Nowak, Sarah, 71–73, 81, 84

Occupational Outlook Handbook (1976; U.S. Department of Labor), 14
Office of New Schools, 100
Of Mice and Men (Steinbeck), 95
Opening the World of Learning (OWL) literacy curriculum, 60
Open Society Institute, 88
organizations changing culture and improving performance, 78–79
outsourcing to lower-wage countries, 9–10
The Overeducated American, 7

parental education, 29, 31–33
parent-child relationships, 28–30
parents managing children's lives, 32–33
Payzant, Thomas, 59
peers
    achievement and behavior of, 41–47
    disruptive behavior, 45–47
    high- *versus* low-income students, 42–47
Pell Grants, 16
Perdomo, Flavia Puello, 81, 101, 102
Perry Preschool Program, 56–57, 67
personal support for students, 97–98
physical facilities, 52
political problems when closing failing schools, 105–106
postsecondary education, 14–15
poverty, 27, 29
prekindergarten programs, 53–69
    Abecedarian Project, 56–57
    acquiring important skills and knowledge, 65–66
    assigning weakest teachers to, 61
    biennial evaluations, 64
    Boston Public Schools (BPS), 58–65
    children from all backgrounds, 68
    cognitive and socioemotional skills, 56
    Head Start, 57
    inequality of, 67
    language skills, 56
    long-term benefits, 68
    mathematics, literacy, and language skills, 58, 66
    parents' work schedules and, 67
    Perry Preschool Program, 56–57
    professionals assisting teachers, 62
    quality and consistency of instruction, 61

school districts, 68
states, 57–58, 67
urban school districts, 57–58
vocabulary and language skills, 64
prekindergarten teachers, 61–64, 66
preschool, center-based, 119–120
primary grades, 40–41
private schools and publicly funded educational vouchers, 132
problem behavior and low-income children, 41
professional development
    activities, 81
    Mott Haven Village Preparatory High School, 102
    as process, 138
    Urban Assembly School for Law and Justice (SLJ), 96
professional parents and words spoken to toddlers, 32
programs
    New Hope program, 110–122
    providing low-income children with opportunities, 3–4
    supporting families, 109–122
promising prekindergarten programs, 53–69
public education
    federal government's strategy to improve, 129–130
    standards-based educational reforms, 38
    states increasing funding for, 127–128
public high schools, 87
publicly funded educational vouchers, 132
public schools
    immigrants participation in civic life, 140
    leveling playing field for children, 2
    meeting challenge, 140–144
    publicly funded educational vouchers, 132
    school districts, 76–77
Puerto Rican immigrants, 35

Raudenbush, Stephen, 73
reading
    achievement gap, 24–25
    building skills, 94–97
    language differences and achievement, 32
    whole-class instruction, 40
reading interview, 72
Red Hook Community Justice Center, 98
Regents examination, 98
remediation, identifying students in need of, 73
residential isolation between high- and low-income families, 41–51

resources, 52
rising academic standards, 37–41
    Common Core State Standards, 38
    requiring students to master more
        sophisticated skills, 38–39
    standards-based educational reforms, 38
Risley, Todd, 31–32
Rodriquez, Josué, 89–90
Rubio, Jose, 85–86, 103–104
Rubio, Mariana, 85–86
Russell, Ben, 62

Sachs, Jason, 59–62, 64–66, 69, 136, 138
Sanchez, John, 90
school achievement
    earnings gains in adulthood, 120–121
    enrichment expenditures, 26–28
    family structure, 31–33
    income and school success, 30–31
    linking income to, 33
    parental education, 31–33
    stress and depression, 28–30
school districts
    organizational structure changes, 130–133
    reform advocates, 131
schooling
    broad and comprehensive definition of, 143
    intergenerational mobility and, 19–21
    widening gulf in outcomes, 15–18
school leaders, 51
    culture of continuous improvement, 141
    improving teaching, 127–128, 141
schools
    accountability, 4, 50, 52, 136–138
    beating the odds, 141
    best way to organize assumptions, 75
    budget controls, 130
    children successful in, 25
    college graduates, 141
    continuing to improve, 77–78
    curricula providing group work, 40
    demonstrating improvement in student
        outcomes, 130
    direct teacher-led instruction, 40
    district administrative structures, 76
    education challenge in twenty-first century,
        75–78
    factors determining success in, 23–24
    funding and improvement, 143
    high- and low-income children gap, 125
    hiring staff, 130
    income and success, 30–31

increased funding for low-income children,
    127–128
initiatives encouraging success, 51–52
instructional achievement, 76
labor force shifts demands on, 38
low-income children's opportunities, 3–4
narrowing curriculum, 129
neglecting skills and areas of knowledge, 129
neighborhood schools, 41
performance gaps, 24–25
reforms, 5
rigid disciplinary policies, 92
segregation by family income, 49, 132, 141
support organizations, 134, 136
supports, 4, 51–52, 134, 136
systems of effective, 141
teaching all students to master skills, 75
School Support Organizations (SSOs), 101–102
secondary education, 8
secretaries, 14
self reliance, 115
service jobs, 10
Settles, Karla, 53–54, 55, 56, 60, 62–63
single-parent family structure, 31
"skill begets skill" hypothesis, 55
skill building, 55
skills needed to earn good living, 125
small high schools, 87
    cutbacks in public funding, 104
    design principles, 98–99
    disadvantaged youth, 87–88
    graduation rate, 103
    long-term relationships with teachers, 101
    not-for-profit groups submitting proposals
        for, 88
    ongoing challenges, 104–106
    personal support for students, 97–98
    political problems when closing failing
        schools, 105–106
    recent immigrants, 89
    request for proposals (RFP), 88–89
    State Regents examination scores, 103
    student evaluation, 103
    support for creation of, 100
    teachers and school leaders burnout,
        104–105
    themes, 98–99
    urban school districts, 107
social inequality, 5
social programs costs and benefits, 120–121
socioeconomic mobility, 124
South Bronx High School, 85
Springfield, Massachusetts, 35

standard of living, 1
standards-based educational reforms, 38
state-mandated tests, 52
states
    alternative accountability systems, 137
    charter schools regulations, 131
    child-care subsidies, 113
    high school graduation requirements, 38–39
    incentive to choose relatively undemanding
        tests, 129
    increasing funding for public education,
        127–128
    low proficiency thresholds, 129
    New Hope program influences, 122
    prekindergarten programs, 57–58, 67
    tests failing to provide valid information
        about student readiness, 129
    waivers from accountability provisions,
        129–130
Strategic Teaching and Evaluation of Progress
    (STEP), 71–72, 78, 81
stress and school achievement, 28–30
students
    critical skills, 75
    higher academic standards, 141
    integrating in classroom, 47–48
    learning affected by achievement and
        behavior of classmates, 41–47
    mastering more sophisticated skills, 38–39
    mobility and academic achievement, 47–48
    personal support for, 97–98
    regular assessment of skills, 73
    remediation, 73
    teaching all to master skills, 75
Study Island software, 72
substance abuse, 29
Success for All (SFA), 82, 83
superintendents tenure in urban school
    districts, 76–77
Supplemental Nutrition Assistance Program,
    140
support, 4, 5
    building systems, 81–83

Tallinger, Garrett, 26, 97, 123
teachers
    ability to control classroom, 45
    access to expertise, 51–52
    accountability, 137
    assignment problem, 47
    attracting and retaining high-quality, 77, 144
    basing transfers on seniority, 77

behavioral expectations, 76
best way to organize work of, 75
classroom management strategies, 76
compensation, 77
effective, 49
high-poverty schools, 49–51, 125
literacy coach, 81
manipulating students' test scores, 129
poor social conditions for work, 142
rules regarding transfers, 50–51
salary schedule, 50
stipends for additional responsibilities, 81–82
students not learning critical skills, 75
variations in methods of teaching, 76
well-educated, 51, 141
Teach for America, 136
teaching
    improving and school leaders, 127–128
    low-income schools, 41
    union contracts, 77
    variations in methods, 76
technological advances, 14
technological changes, 9
teenagers unemployment rate, 7
telecommunications, 9–10
Temporary Assistance for Needy Families
    Program, 110
test-based accountability, 126, 128–130
TIDE (Topic Sentence, Introduce Evidence,
    Discuss Evidence) strategy, 96
Title I funds, 127–128
transistors, 7
The Trumpet of the Swan (White), 3
Tulsa schools, 68

Uncommon Schools, 80, 131
unemployment rate, 7
union contracts, 77
unionized jobs, 14
unions and New Century High Schools, 88
United Federation of Teachers, 88
United Kingdom upward economic mobility,
    21
universal secondary education, 8
University of Chicago
    charter management organization (CMO),
        73, 81–82
    Strategic Teaching and Evaluation of
        Progress (STEP), 81
    Urban Education Institute (EUI), 77–78, 128
University of Chicago Charter School network,
    71, 73, 137

academic skills evaluations, 73–74
advances in knowledge, 138
afterschool tutors, 78
campuses, 73
increasing funding for, 128
lessons from, 80–82
management support for, 80
per pupil expenditures, 74
reading and mathematical skills, 74
recruiting teachers, 78
small network of schools, 74
strategies to improve education in high-
     poverty schools, 74–75
systems of schools continuing to improve,
     77–78
Urban Education Institute (UEI), 73
upper-middle-class families
enrichment expenditures, 26–28
parental support for adolescents, 97
upward mobility, 2, 133
Urban Assembly School for Law and Justice
     (SLJ), 86, 93–94, 136, 137
assessing student's readiness for college, 102
criminal justice system, 98
English Language Arts, 95
Forensics class, 95
funding and activities cutbacks, 104
grade-level meetings, 95–96
increasing funding for, 128
Independent Reading, 95
instruction building on students' skills, 96
law and justice theme, 93–94
literacy skills, 139
master teachers, 96
personal support for students, 97
professional development, 96
reading skills, 94–97
Regents English examination, 96
school report card, 101
students and advisors, 94
summer melt research, 139
teachers and school leaders burnout, 104–105
TIDE (Topic Sentence, Introduce Evidence,
     Discuss Evidence) strategy, 96
visiting colleges, 98
Urban Education Institute (UEI), 73, 77–78, 128
urban school districts, 76
building support systems, 80–83
bureaucracies in departments, 77
lack of funding, 80
prekindergarten programs, 57–58, 68
professional development activities, 81
reading skills assessments, 81

recruiting and preparing school leaders, 81
small high schools, 107
superintendents' tenure, 76–77
teen safety, 92
union contracts, 77
University of Chicago Charter School
     network, 80–82
U.S. Department of Education alternative
     accountability provisions, 130
U.S. Department of Labor, 14
U.S. District Court, 98

Vera Institute of Justice, 98
violence, exposure to, 27
voucher programs, 132

Weiland, Christina, 66
welfare-recipient families
enrichment expenditures, 26–28
number of words spoken to toddlers, 32
welfare reform, 112–114
Minnesota, 119
Wellesley Centers for Women, 59, 69
biennial evaluations of prekindergarten
     system, 64
classroom evaluations, 62
classroom observations, 65
Weschler, Norman, 89
White, E.B., 3
white-collar occupations, 13–14
whole-class instruction for reading, 40
Williams, Alexander, 12–13, 23, 97, 123
Wilson, Steven, 79–80
workers
decline in earnings without postsecondary
     education, 14–15
demand for highly-educated, 9
educating, 1
with less education, 8–9, 15
working-class families
enrichment expenditures, 26–28
financial stability, 10–11
number of words spoken to toddlers, 32
working-class urban neighborhood, 10

Yoshikawa, Hiro, 66

Zajac, Christine, 35–37, 42–45, 46, 47, 75
Zucker, Stefan, 90, 92